Radio Journalism

Radio Journalism

JOHN R. BITTNER
DePauw University

DENISE A. BITTNER
WGRE-FM

PRENTICE-HALL, INC., ENGLEWOOD CLIFFS, NEW JERSEY 07632

Library of Congress Cataloging in Publication Data

BITTNER, JOHN R. (date)
  Radio journalism.

  (Prentice-Hall series in speech communication)
  Includes index.
  1. Radio journalism. I. Bittner, Denise A., (date) joint author. II. Title.
PN4784.R2B5   070.1′9   76-29048
ISBN 0-13-750463-2
ISBN 0-13-750455-1 pbk.

PRINTED IN THE UNITED STATES OF AMERICA

10 9 8 7 6 5 4 3 2 1

Prentice-Hall Speech Communication Series

Larry Barker and Robert Kibler, *Editors*

PRENTICE-HALL INTERNATIONAL, INC., *London*
PRENTICE-HALL OF AUSTRALIA PTY. LIMITED, *Sydney*
PRENTICE-HALL OF CANADA LTD., *Toronto*
PRENTICE-HALL OF INDIA PRIVATE LIMITED, *New Delhi*
PRENTICE-HALL OF JAPAN, INC., *Tokyo*
PRENTICE-HALL OF SOUTHEAST ASIA PTE. LTD., *Singapore*
WHITEHALL BOOKS LIMITED, *Wellington, New Zealand*

For Our Parents:
Gwen and Earl
Dorothy and Smokey

Contents

3   *News Sources*   *33*

4   *Covering Radio News*   *51*

Preface

Radio news is the vibrant part of a dynamic medium. In America alone, over 8,000 radio stations comprise a system that carries the news to more people faster than any other medium. Internationally, thousands more provide the same service. In fact, it's the first source of news every day for a majority of the world's population. Radio, the oldest form of broadcast news reporting, is now experiencing unprecedented growth and increased professionalism. To meet this surge, new national radio news networks are emerging, as are state and regional radio news networks. In addition, FM radio news is flourishing, with no end in sight.

This book is about the practice of radio journalism. It can serve as a main text for a course in broadcast journalism and a supplemental text for students enrolled in such courses as basic reporting, broadcast writing, broadcast management, radio announcing, or general courses dealing with mass communication and journalism. It's for students who aspire to a career in radio journalism. It's for working professionals who want to review practices which may have become habit or been forgotten. It's also for advertising and public relations professionals who need to understand what radio journalism is all about.

Acknowledgments

Many people are part of this book, and they deserve our sincere appreciation. Without placing one ahead of another, we would like to thank the professionals with whom one or both of us have had the pleasure of working. Hal Youart, Tom Brown, Carl Anderson, Pat Nugent, Ed Willis, Paul Evans, Ray Eppel, and Monk Johnson all contributed support, knowledge, and understanding. John DeCamp and Matt Campbell made a recommendation to two employers that started one of us on a career; Bob Krueger and Beverly Green provided the opportunity, encouragement, and enthusiasm for the other career. Bill Ketter and John (Nick) Gregory lived through the thick of professional experiences, as did Boyd Gill, Jerry Lebo, Hortense Myers, Kurt Freudenthal, LeRoy Adams, and John Payne.

We also express our gratitude to the Department of Communication at Purdue University and the School of Journalism at the University of Oregon. And certainly, those students who challenged our thoughts and set the fires of new ideas deserve a very special mention.

Critical reviews by Robert Avery, Lewis O'Donnell, and Robert Weiss are much appreciated. Also, Glenn Starlin suggested important material to include in the book. We especially thank the people at Prentice-Hall, Inc. for professional encouragement and belief in the book, and we also thank Jackie Baumann for her help in typing the manuscript.

Radio Journalism

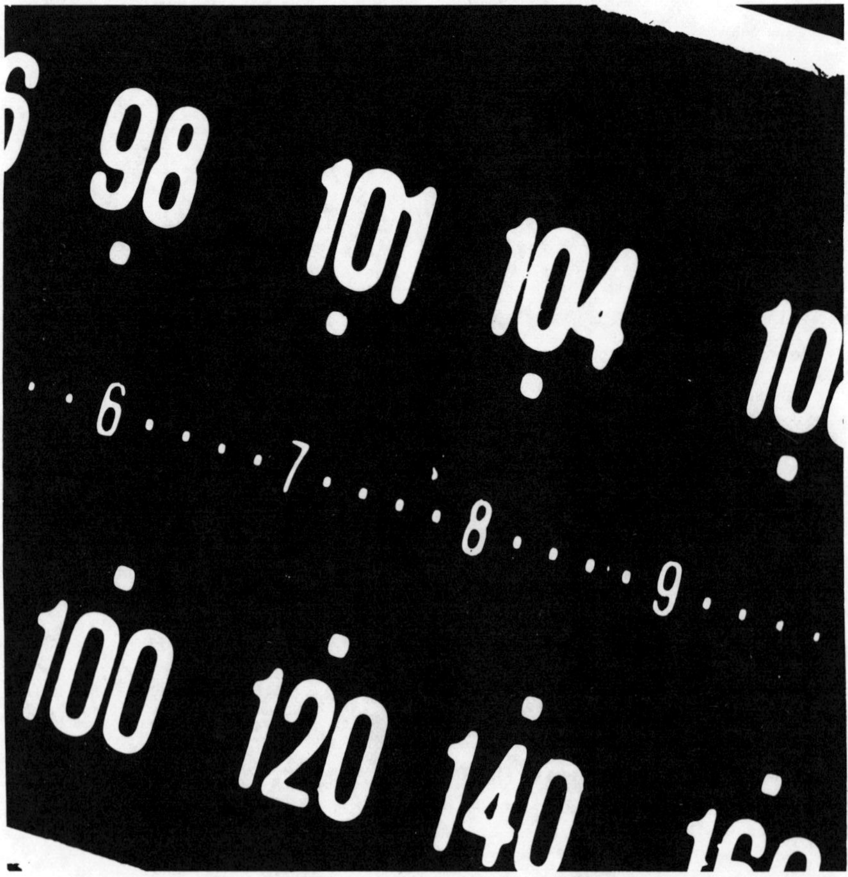
98
101
104
6
7
8
9
100
120
140

chapter one

Radio:
An Emerging Consciousness

"But first, if this broadcast is reaching you, please drop us a card. Address station KDKA, Westinghouse, Pittsburgh, Pennsylvania."

With those words, radio began its first major news broadcast to the American public—the November, 1920 Harding-Cox Presidential election returns.

Over the next fifty years, this new medium would transform the structure of society and shrink the globe. It would record the applause for flying ace Charles Lindberg as President Calvin Coolidge presented him to Congress after his historic New York-to-Paris flight. It would report the inauguration of President Franklin D. Roosevelt, the explosion of the Hindenburg dirigible, the funeral of King George V, the abdication of the English throne by Edward the VIII for the woman he loved, Hitler's declaration of war on Poland, the D-Day invasions, the election of America's first Catholic president and his tragic assassination, and the sound of man's voice from the surface of the moon. It would bring news to more people with greater speed than any other medium. Radio would come of age and survive the challenges of television to become the most pervasive medium in the world today.

THE EARLY YEARS

Although KDKA became the first commercially licensed radio station to broadcast news, it by no means cornered the radio news market. In fact, simultaneously with the KDKA broadcast, the *Detroit News* station, 8MK, broadcast the Harding-Cox election returns on its "experimental" radio devices. Station 8MK had even broadcast results of the Michigan primary election returns three months earlier. But while 8MK's purpose was to lure listeners into reading the *Detroit News*, station KDKA's purpose was its own survival as a new medium.

The idea of voices over airwaves was not new to America; the concept had intrigued Alexander Graham Bell as early as 1876. It was not until 1901, however, that the idea became reality. A Canadian engineer, Reginald Fessenden, developed the concept of "continuous airwaves," an enormous improvement over Guglielmo Marconi's "airwave bursts" of translated dots and dashes.[1] In 1906 Fessenden experimented with these waves by broadcasting a Christmas Eve program of instrumentals, vocal selections and poetry readings. Ships at sea receiving the broadcast responded immediately to the "wireless voice." Letters poured in requesting more of "everything in general" and "news in particular." Using the concept of Fessenden's continuous airwaves, the Marconi station at South Wellfleet on Cape Cod began broadcasting news to ships several times a day, and a steamer company on the Great Lakes even contracted with the Tomas E. Clark Wireless Telegraph and Telephone Company to receive 1906 election returns.[2]

Then in April of 1912, America held its breath as a lone wireless reporter broadcast for seventy-two uninterrupted hours the tragic sinking of the *U.S.S. Titanic*. The reporter was twenty-one-year-old David Sarnoff, who contacted rescue ships, gathered surviver lists, and attracted attention to radio as a responsible and dynamic informational medium. Sarnoff later became president of the Radio Corporation of America (RCA).

This new informational role of radio so impressed President Woodrow Wilson that he chose the medium on January 8, 1918 to broadcast his famous Fourteen Points, a primary influence in inducing Germany's surrender in World War I. Radio carried Wilson's speech to the doorsteps of Berlin.[3]

By the 1920s radio journalism was exploring new horizons with analyses of world situations by a single commentator and live broadcasts of controversial social issues. WGN in Chicago, at the then enormous cost of $1,000 per day in telephone line charges, broadcast the 1925 Scopes trial, in which a teacher, John Thomas Scopes, was accused of the "crime" of teaching evolution. The emotions of two debating attorneys, Clarence Darrow and William Jennings Bryan, penetrated the American living room with the dialogue:

[1] Erik Barnouw, *Tower of Babel: A History of Broadcasting in the United States to 1933* (New York: Oxford University Press, 1966), I, 19.
[2] *Ibid.*, pp. 29, 34.
[3] *Ibid.*, p. 51.

BRYAN: I want the world to know that this man, who does not believe in God, is trying to use a court in Tennessee—

DARROW: I object to that!

BRYAN: —to slur at it, and while it will require time, I am willing to take it!

DARROW: I object to your statement! I am examining you on your fool ideas that no intelligent Christian on Earth believes! [4]

Radio news had truly become the "personal medium."

THE NETWORKS BEGIN

The expense of the Scopes Trial broadcast placed new emphasis on a serious problem. A virtual monopoly on cable hookups by American Telephone and Telegraph Company was creating soaring costs in long distance broadcast lines. Independent stations like WGN that were not owned by AT&T had to lease telephone lines in order to transmit over long distances. Alternative transmission hookups, such as short-wave links and telegraph wires, were available but inadequate. Disputes involving competing RCA, Westinghouse Corporation and General Electric company-owned radio stations provoked Congressional hearings, with Secretary of Commerce Herbert Hoover playing a key negotiating role. The compromises resulting from these disputes signaled the emergence of a radio network owned cooperatively by RCA, Westinghouse, and G. E. and contracting AT&T's telephone wires. The year was 1926, and the network was the National Broadcasting Company. Radio news could now be distributed by a national network to almost any station that wanted it.

By January of 1927, NBC had two networks in operation, the Red Network and the Blue Network. NBC utilized them to cover the 1927 Rose Bowl Game, which became America's first transcontinental network broadcast. However, this exclusivity was short-lived, and in April of 1927 a second company appeared. It was CBS, the Columbia Broadcasting System.

With the added flavor of competition plus the financial and personnel advantages of networks, radio news reporting thrived. The year 1927 introduced listeners to the first multiple-announcer radio broadcast, in which successive NBC announcers described Charles Lindbergh's returning ticker-tape parade through the streets of New York City.[5]

In 1931 CBS launched a weekly radio news series that bordered on entertainment. Called the "March of Time" and sponsored by *Time* magazine,

[4] John Fink, *WGN: A Pictorial History* (Chicago: WGN, Inc., 1961), p. 22.
[5] Barnouw, *Tower of Babel*, p. 192.

the series reenacted the major news of the week with actors, sound effects, and an entire dramatic production. CBS also experimented with new techniques of legitimate radio news broadcasting; these included reporting events from moving trains, from balloons, and even from a bathysphere twenty-two hundred feet under water. The CBS announcer held an audience spellbound with the exciting underwater description, "It is absolutely black. Now there are fish two or three feet away . . . It is the most amazing thing now . . . Here come loads of little—I don't know what they are. I've never seen anything like them." [6]

Despite the surging progress of the new medium, radio news still lacked an important element—its own news-gathering organization. As late as 1932, radio still depended primarily upon newspapers or wire services for information. That came to an end in April, 1933 when the Associated Press refused to provide radio networks with news; the only exceptions were radio stations owned by Associated Press papers. These were favored by short news bulletins, but the stations had to pay for them. United Press and the International News Service quickly followed with their own radio news blackouts. Their purpose was to eliminate the threat of competition to newspapers. Radio news had been drawing national attention with its spectacular achievements—attention newspapers wanted to snuff out. But the blackout idea backfired when, in the fall of 1933, NBC and CBS began gathering their own news, ceasing their total reliance on the wire services.

The one-man news team of A. A. ("Abe") Schechter picked up the phone at NBC and started a radio news-gathering operation that shook the competition. Schechter scooped story after story from both wire services and newspapers, providing news not only for NBC's weekday Lowell Thomas program, but also for NBC's weekend Walter Winchell gossip/ news program.[7] Not to be outdone, CBS launched an even more elaborate news-gathering organization. Spearheaded by former United Press editor Paul W. White, the network organized a nationwide corps of correspondents, mainly freelance "stringers," and paid them for news stories actually aired on CBS. In addition, White negotiated news exchange procedures with overseas news operations.[8]

Feeling threatened, the newspapers staged a publicity boycott of network programs. When matters became critical in December, 1933, a compromise emerged between print and broadcast organizations. Named the *Biltmore Program,* the pact established these agreements: (1) CBS would abandon its news service; (2) NBC would cease developing its news-gathering operation; (3) a Press-Radio Bureau would be established at radio net-

<hr>

[6] "The Way We've Been . . . And Are," *Columbine,* 2, No. 7 (April/May 1974), 1.
[7] Erik Barnouw, *The Golden Web: A History of Broadcasting in the United States from 1933 to 1953* (New York: Oxford University Press, 1968), II, 19.
[8] *Ibid.,* p. 20.

work expense to supply thirty-word bulletins from AP, UP and INS, to be aired during hours that would ensure newspapers "scoop" protection and would refer listeners to the newspapers for additional information; (4) radio commentators would be limited to providing background information and would be prohibited from utilizing news less than twelve hours old; and (5) commercial sponsorship of these news bureau bulletins would be prohibited. Newspapers, in return, would end their radio publicity boy-cott.[9]

Radio news, however, still had a card up its sleeve—independent radio news services. One of these mavericks, Transradio, survived, thrived, and broke rule after rule of the *Biltmore Program*. Radio stations using such news services began to prosper under commercial sponsorship. Finally, UP and INS began to sell their news to radio, followed quickly by AP. The Press-Radio Bureau became insignificant when rumblings of Hitler in Europe pushed network radio news-gathering into the forefront again. Radio news overcame the challenge triumphantly. In fact, out of this challenge arose still another radio network, the Mutual Broadcasting System in 1934.

Radio subsequently brought the voice of President Franklin Delano Roosevelt into the American home twenty times in his first nine months in office. Roosevelt realized the enormous impact of this personal medium and utilized it in his famous "fireside chats."

Radio became the vehicle to communicate dramatic moments in history to the American public. It captured the voice of reporter Herb Morrison reacting with shock and horror as the Hindenburg dirible burst into flames before his eyes. With his voice strained by the tragedy, Morrison gasped these descriptions to his radio audience:

> It burst into flames! It's crashing, it's crashing—terrible—oh my— Get out of the way please—
>
> It's burning, bursting into flames and its falling on the mooring stands and all the folks agree that—
>
> This is terrible, this is one of the worst catastrophes that the world— Eoh— it's—
>
> Four- or five-hundred feet into the sky and it's, it's a terrific crash, ladies and gentlemen—
>
> The smoke and the flames now, and the fires are crashing to the ground, not quite to the mooring mast—
>
> Oh the humanity and all the passengers—
>
> I don't even—

[9] Llewellyn White, *Commissions on Freedom of the Press: The American Radio* (Chicago: The University of Chicago Press, 1947), p. 45.

I can't talk to people whose friends are on there!

It's, it's, it's, oh—

I can't talk, ladies and gentlemen!

Honest, it's a mass of flaming, smoking wreckage, and everybody can hardly breathe and talk at the same—

Lady, lady, I'm sorry—

Honest, I, I can hardly breathe!

I'm going to step inside where I cannot see it!

I'm telling you that's terrible.

I—I—

Listen folks, I'm going to have to stop a minute because I've lost my voice. This is the worst thing I've ever witnessed!

Radio news also brought European voices into America's living rooms. With his deep British voice stating, "I have found it impossible to carry the heavy burden of responsibility and to discharge my duties as King as I would wish to do without the help and support of the woman I love," King Edward VIII abdicated the throne in 1937.

With such direct and exciting presentation of the news, it's no wonder that people had come to rely more on radio news as a believable source than on the medium of newspapers, as a *Fortune* magazine poll showed in 1939.[10]

WARTIME RADIO NEWS

World War II saw radio news leap forward again. This time it leaped into the monumental responsibility of world politics and voluntary censorship. New radio news forms emerged, such as the *news roundups* created by Edward R. Murrow, European director for CBS. With the words "I return you now to . . . ," CBS reporters from Vienna, London, Paris, Berlin, Rome, and New York were all heard on the same newscast.[11] Radio news style also made the transition during this era from written journalism into spoken journalism.

Another unique approach developed through the utilization of war commentators, who were assigned to interpret European happenings as they saw them. However, some war commentators took advantage of their assignment to advocate personal viewpoints. Such action prompted enormous political clashes between the commentators, the government, and the American public, clashes which became so severe that CBS introduced the term *news*

[10] "The Press and the People—A Survey," *Fortune*, 20, No. 2 (August 1939), 65.
[11] Barnouw, *The Golden Web*, p. 78.

analyst to replace *commentator*. According to CBS, an analyst was to analyze the news, not promote a personal viewpoint. The National Association of Broadcasters established similar "personal viewpoint" guidelines for radio news broadcasts in 1939. Such guidelines were to emerge in legal form in the historic 1941 "Mayflower Doctrine," which in essence states that a truly free radio cannot be an advocate.[12]

World War II thrust radio news into a delicate situation—voluntary censorship of news. To monitor this campaign, the United States government created the Office of Censorship and named Byron Price of the Associated Press as its director, with an assistant director, John Harold Ryan, in charge of radio. Under the guidelines established by Ryan and Price, this massive voluntary experiment worked fairly well. The only major crisis occurred when a Mutual Broadcasting System reporter told listeners on his "Confidentially Yours" series that Pasco, Washington was the site of an atomic research project. Furious, military leaders demanded that voluntary censorship be replaced with military censorship, but the voluntary system survived intact.[13]

The war years saw a fourth radio broadcasting company evolve. In 1943 NBC sold its Blue Network to American Broadcasting System, Inc., who renamed the network ABC.

THE POSTWAR CHANGES

Just when radio news seemed to be thriving, World War II ended, and the massive daily influx of news suddenly stopped. Television news posed a serious threat, as did the burgeoning cost of rapidly changing radio equipment. Thus, radio news was forced to develop what became known as the "rip and read" news style, by which wire service ticker-tape machines provided information at low cost and transformed disk jockeys into pseudo-journalists.

When television emerged as a significant medium, radio faced another challenge—a shrinking listening audience for network programming. Starting in the late 1950s, the thrust of radio changed. The emphasis became "local radio" rather than "national radio." Ironically for radio journalism, the television threat turned out to be a blessing in disguise. When many entertainment programs on radio networks fizzled, the networks focused instead on news. But the medium still faced the problem of reaching the specialized local audience.

---

[12] *In the Matter of the Mayflower Broadcasting Corporation and the Yankee Network, Inc. (WAAB)*, 8 FCC 333, 338 (Jan. 16, 1941).
[13] Barnouw, *The Golden Web*, p. 157.

DEMOGRAPHIC NETWORKS DEVELOP

Radio network management was not immune to trends emerging in the broadcasting industry. These people saw the success of network television. They recognized that individual radio stations could make a greater profit from local commercials than from network income and were consequently dropping their network affiliations. They were also finding it hard to convince advertisers wanting to reach a specialized audience, such as teenagers, to buy commercials on national radio, which geared its programming to general audiences. The advertiser realized that it was much more economical to place selected commercials on only those radio stations that reached the teenage audience. Ultimately, management realized it needed to drastically reorganize the radio networks in order to save them.

ABC Pioneers the Split

On January 1, 1968, ABC split its network radio into four distinct entities—American Contemporary Radio Network, American FM Radio Network, American Entertainment Radio Network, and American Information Network. Each had its own specialized content, format, delivery, and sound.

This move by ABC caught much of the broadcasting industry off guard. Criticism from industry people charged that the move wasn't really a split, and the four networks weren't actually independent of each other. The Mutual Broadcasting System pleaded repeatedly before the Federal Communications Commission (FCC) to have the four-network concept blocked as a monopoly. However, the action failed to influence the Commission, and the four-network concept survived. For ABC, it was truly a new dimension in network programming. It was the first time radio news had made a specific effort to reach the specialized audiences that local radio had already been serving.

ABC based its concept on audience *demographics* (age, sex, education, income, etc.). Each of the four ABC networks tailored its news presentation to fit a particular audience. For example, a young contemporary station might previously have shied away from the traditional radio news network because it was not considered attractive to its target audience. Traditional news did not provide the shorter newscasts, contemporary delivery, or contemporary outlook to satisfactorily blend with the musical format of the station. ABC could now offer this station a happy solution—American Contemporary Radio Network.

Moreover, the typical young audience that listened to the contemporary format presented a well-defined market for advertisers. Advertisers could now purchase commercials on the Contemporary Network to reach that specific audience, thereby "zeroing in" on their market. To reach a different type of audience, they could purchase commercials on the ABC Entertainment Radio Network, which geared its news programming to stations featuring a middle-of-the-road (MOR) format, music that ranged somewhere between rock and classical.

A series of ads in the early 1970s characterized the thrust of ABC's demographic concept. One such ad for the American Information Radio Network, based on a W. R. Simmons, Inc. study, listed seven different demographic characteristics—age, education, marital status, occupation, income range, price of home, and the number and ages of children. The ad then stated:

> If you're an advertiser who wants to reach affluent thoughtful Americans, we have 470 stations beamed straight at them. The American Information Radio Network.

Directed toward potential advertisers, this ad described in alluring detail the type of audience the commercial announcements would reach via the American Information Radio Network.

Each of the ABC networks supplied news to its affiliates at a different time of the hour, never overlapping; thus ABC could use a *single* leased telephone line to each market instead of four separate lines. ABC could also have more than one network in a market, a distinct advantage. Whereas other networks, under FCC monopoly restrictions, could place only one affiliate in a market, ABC could now place four separate affiliates per market.

Ethnic Radio News: More Competition

The civil rights movement of the 1960s focused new attention on minority cultures. America began to recognize the unique qualities of its black Americans, Indians, Hispanic-Americans, Orientals, and others. Although no one had ever questioned the need to direct programming at the young radio audience, programmers rarely thought about orienting programming to various ethnic audiences. All of these attitudes began to change. Radio stations oriented toward the black audience began to emerge, and soul music introduced by soul disc jockeys appeared in major markets throughout the country. Soon every major city not only had its own rock station and good music station, but also its own black and Spanish stations.

Mutual became the first to apply the network concept to these ethnic audiences. It announced in 1971 that it was joining the multinetwork ranks by adding to its already existing MBS network the Mutual Black Network and the Mutual Spanish Network. Mutual based this plan on ethnic demographics and designed news programming specifically for black and Spanish audiences. However, Mutual decided to disband its Spanish network after several months of operation. Instead of finding an audience united by an ethnic background, the network found three distinctively different groups of Spanish-speaking Americans with no common denominator among them for news authenticity. The East Coast Hispanic-Americans, for example, who were of Puerto Rican descent, had different problems and interests from the Florida Hispanic-Americans, who were of Cuban descent. They, in turn, had different problems and interests from the Southwest and West Coast Hispanic-Americans, who were of Mexican descent.

ABC reacted to Mutual's decision to direct newscasts to ethnic audiences by announcing in August of 1971 that it would provide affiliates with a weekly service of minority news features. The year 1973 saw still another minority network take to the air, the independently owned and operated National Black Network, which provided hourly newscasts geared to the black audience.

In 1973 Mutual added a fourth network to compete with the American Contemporary Radio Network. Labeled the Mutual Progressive Network, it oriented its news to stations whose musical programming leaned more toward progressive rock than toward MÓR or Top-40. Moreover, Mutual made the service available to educational stations in markets that had no existing Mutual affiliate.

NBC emerged with a new radio network in 1975, the News and Information Service (NIS). NIS took advantage of a trend toward the three-hour morning drive-time blocks of radio news that were becoming popular in major markets. It introduced an all-news programming format with fifty minutes of network news every hour, much more than the typical five minutes of news provided each hour by other networks. NIS required affiliates to accept at least thirty minutes of its news; the rest was up to the affiliates. Although adoption of this new network came slowly, when the first results showed how well NIS stations fared in their markets, business boomed. For the data revealed that not only did NIS cut stations' costs by eliminating the need for expensive news personnel, but it also boosted their ratings, sometimes as much as 700 percent for certain target audiences.

Wire Service Audio News

Along with the radio networks, UPI and AP also formed services to provide live audio news reports. UPI started a service in 1968 called UPI Audio. AP followed in 1974 with a service called AP Radio. UPI and AP did not regard their services as networks in the traditional sense; subscribing stations could edit the newscasts as they pleased, or even delay individual broadcasts. Unlike network broadcasts which carried commercials, the UPI and AP audio services didn't. Thus, affiliates could sell their own commercials in each of the newscasts. Moreover, stations were not "required" to carry the newscasts. In addition, AP Radio provided news from specific regions of the country. Stations in the Southeast and Northeast, Midwest and Southwest, Mountain and Pacific regions received a series of regional audio news stories they could incorporate into local programming. Like the networks, both wire services also provided such features as sports, business news, and live coverage of major events.

National Public Radio

In 1971, the Corporation for Public Broadcasting (CPB), a federally funded corporation, developed the National Public Radio Network (NPR) for publicly-owned radio stations. Many of these stations are found on college and university campuses and are financed by public contributions. NPR has gained a reputation for carrying extended live coverage of various congressional hearings and for the production of its award-winning daily network news and features roundup, "All Things Considered." Much of the listenership of public radio stations consists of college-educated people. Although the penetration of the network is not yet extensive, it is steadily increasing. Legislation to provide long term funding of the CPB will undoubtedly aid the development of NPR, enabling it to become a more effective competitor with the major commercial networks.

REGIONAL NETWORKS DEVELOP

Although national networks provide a major service to affiliate stations and listeners, many stations also want to increase their coverage of regional news and news of other cities in their state, especially the state capital.

State Networks

In response to this need, stations in some areas of the country have successfully initiated regional radio news networks. Illinois and Indiana are two states that have active state news networks. The Illinois network, known as the Illinois News Network (INN), and the Indiana Broadcasters Association News Network (IBANN) both have a main office located in their respective state capitals. Typical of other state networks, the IBANN system functions as a cooperative, with subscriber stations contributing *audio actualities,* which are the actual sounds of news recorded on tape, from their respective areas of the state. Full-time IBANN reporters cover news of the capital city of Indianapolis. Subscriber stations can record any or all of this news by calling the central IBANN number in Indianapolis.

A problem for this system and other cooperatives is the hesitancy felt by some stations to send stories to IBANN, thus making them available to their competitors. To try to alleviate this problem, IBANN initiated an awards competition and installed a toll-free line for subscribing members. Another problem of such a system is that, because it relies so heavily upon news from its subscribers, it is only as good as the subscribers make it. Nevertheless, the desire on the part of the stations to have regional radio news actualities has kept the system running effectively.

Similar systems ranging from complete regularly scheduled newscasts to a set of audio actualities for use in local news programming are beginning to function in other areas of the country. Wire service audio network management is keeping a close watch on the progress of such operations, indicating that the future may bring the development of still more regional wire service audio news networks. Because of this nation-wide interest, the National Association of State Radio Networks (NASRN) came into being to foster the continued development of state network systems. Currently, NASRN has member networks in Texas, Arkansas, Missouri, Georgia, Maine, Indiana, Louisiana, and Oklahoma.

Educational Networks

The development of state television networks for transmitting educational television (ETV) and instructional television (ITV) to college campuses has led to the development of state radio networks linking college radio stations. In these systems, television transmission lines, and in some cases microwave hookups, of the state ETV-ITV television networks are made available to campus radio stations. These facilities are then used to deliver regularly scheduled newscasts, exchange audio actualities, or in some cases carry regularly scheduled radio news programming from commercial networks that have cooperative arrangements with the state ETV-ITV network. For the campus station, such a system provides the opportunity to receive and disseminate news of general interest to student audiences. A problem can result when campus stations are closely associated with the public relations function of their school administration, rather than being a truly independent news voice of their community. In these cases, the true journalistic function of the entire system can diminish to a diet of public relations. Where used properly, however, such systems provide an opportunity for students to gain practical experience working with a radio network.

Informal Networks

In addition to formally established news networks, informal networks also exist among radio journalists. In most cases, such networks result from personal associations that grow until groups of perhaps five or more stations share correspondent reports and audio actualities on a regular basis.

IMPACT AND FUTURE DIMENSIONS

The impact of radio has increased steadily since the early 1920s, when listeners crowded around crystal sets to hear the latest election returns. Moreover, the growing national desire to "be informed," and be informed "on the run," has increased the importance of the medium as a prime disseminator of news.

A major factor contributing to radio's impact has been the constant miniaturization of radio components, making it the most mobile medium in the world, one which brings news of Washington and Moscow to the driver of an automobile on a crowded American freeway. This mobility, especially during crisis situations such as earthquakes, floods, or tornadoes, makes radio a unique source of news and emergency instructions. In fact, radio commands the attention of the public during a crisis and is relied upon as a central information clearing house even more than the local police department.

The recent prosperity of the medium has contributed to the success of radio journalism. For instance, the operating costs of a radio station are far less than those of a television station. Eliminated from radio is the cost of such expensive equipment as color portable transmission systems, cameras, videotape recorders and antenna, and microwave dishes needed for on-the-spot transmission of televised news. For the radio journalist, a nearby telephone is all that is needed to link an event anywhere in the world with an international network of listeners. This low overhead has permitted responsible radio managers to spend increased revenues on local news.

A look at research data showing radio's penetration clearly indicates the medium's importance. For example, a RADAR (Radio's All Dimension Audience Research) study shows 159 million Americans listen to radio every week, or more than 96 percent of everyone twelve years of age and older.[14] Pulse, Inc. figures show FM set penetration increasing at the

[14] "Radio Continues to be Everywhere," *Broadcasting*, 86, No. 21 (May 27, 1974), 36-37.

rate of as much as 10 percent a year.[15] Advertising agency Ogilvy & Mather's fifth edition Pocket Guide to media listed the average number of sets per household at 5.4 in 1974. A report issued by the Radio Advertising Bureau (RAB) based on Simmons, Inc. research shows 94 percent of adult males in households with annual incomes of $25,000 or more listen to radio, and 89 percent of adult males in households with annual incomes between $15,000 and $24,999 listen to radio. The trend clearly shows radio listening increases with income, an important consideration for advertisers wanting to reach the high-income buyer. Research data released by RAB from a Trendex survey cast additional light on the medium's ability to reach the population as the first and predominant source of news. The survey's data indicate radio is the major news medium for the majority of awake hours for most individuals.

A 1974 public opinion poll commissioned by CBS Radio by the Opinion Research Corporation showed that radio was the primary source of morning news for 57 percent of those surveyed, while television was the first morning news source for 19 percent, and newspapers for 18 percent. The survey also found that among persons eighteen to twenty-nine years of age, 59 percent chose radio, as did 58 percent of persons thirty to thirty-nine years of age. Sixty-one percent of people in the $15,000 and over family income category chose radio as their primary source of news in the morning.[16]

Additional research in scholarly journals and trade publications confirms radio's growth and its importance as a news source to a mobile and sophisticated public. Others predict the growth of cable radio with nationwide systems much like television. Many cable television corporations currently carry radio programming on one or more of their television channels. The increase in international communication can result in cooperative international radio networks much like American networks.

This increased importance of the medium calls for a new type of radio journalist, one who is bred neither from the background of television nor of newspapers, but from the audio medium. This new radio journalist will need to understand the complexities, peculiarities, and unique qualities of the medium, which are distinct and separate from both print and video communication. Modern radio journalists will need to communicate with the total force of a medium that demands the involvement, imagination and active participation of its listeners. The most imperative of the radio journalist's qualities, however, will be the ability to use the medium responsibly. Whenever an opportunity exists to use the imagination, the

[15] "Onward and Upward in FM Penetration," *Broadcasting,* 87, No. 1 (July 1, 1974), 28.
[16] "Radio Grows as First News Source of Day," *Broadcasting,* 87, No. 9 (August 26, 1974), 23.

potential also lurks for that imagination to stretch beyond the bounds of factual reality. Responsible communication of news and information that employs the extraordinary advantages of radio will be what the radio journalist, uniquely trained, brings to the future of electronic journalism. These unique aspects of radio journalism are what the following chapters will examine.

SUMMARY

When radio news first crackled onto the airwaves, it created a new press that was to revolutionize the entire concept of news. Radio brought the actual sounds of news into the living room and brought them there at the exact moment when that news was happening. Radio networks enabled news to be broadcast from one end of the country to another and established radio news-gathering operations to facilitate these continental broadcasts.

After surviving the unique reporting and voluntary censorship requirements of World War II, radio news suddenly found itself in jeopardy. Television had garnered much of radio's audience, forcing radio programming to become specialized. Radio news programming followed suit. Consequently today we can flip our radio dial and find not only music suited to our tastes, but also news geared to our interests, locality, and even our ethnic origin.

The miniaturization of radio components has given radio vast mobility, making it the predominant news source for an on-the-go population.

SUGGESTED EXERCISES

1. Visit a radio station in your community. Discuss with the general manager the historical background of the station.
2. Monitor five different radio stations. Compare the local and national news programming of each. How do they differ?
3. Interview the news director of a radio station in your community. Determine what networks or wire services serve the station.
4. Visit the headquarters of your local telephone company. Ask how news programs generated by radio networks are transmitted via telephone company facilities to local stations.
5. Talk with people you know who reached adulthood by the year 1935. Ask them to tell you their impressions of radio news programs they listened to in the early years of radio.

chapter two

Ethics
and Responsibilities

People are subject to human error, human emotion, and human failure, and radio journalism must contend with these shortcomings. No machine and no technology can guarantee *absolute* accuracy and objectivity in the process of news-gathering and reporting. Despite the fact that we attempt to attain these goals, they are ideals, not always reality.

It is not the purpose of this chapter to establish moral and ethical principles by which radio journalists can function; that is impossible for any text. In the end, the individual determines those matters, not a book. This chapter does, however, provide some examples to foster intelligent and perceptive exploration of the ethics and responsibilities that every radio journalist must face.

ACCURACY

The importance of accuracy in radio journalism is fundamental. Obviously, a station that does not strive to be accurate will quickly lose its credibility and its listenership.

The most elementary form of accuracy concerns obtaining the basic facts when a reporter is assigned to cover and write a radio news story. For example, a story about an automobile accident in which two people were killed produces bits of related information. The radio reporter assigned to cover such a story learns the names of the individuals, their ages, home town, facts on how the accident happened, and whether any laws were violated. These facts are then written into a composite story and broadcast.

How Situations Affect Accuracy

To gain a better perspective on the concept of accuracy, imagine you are the reporter assigned to cover this same fatality accident. How do you gather the information for your story?

Perhaps you hear about the accident on the police monitor. You then call the desk sergeant at police headquarters, and she informs you of the exact location of the accident. Next, you drive to the scene and interview one of the investigating officers. You return to the radio station, type your story, insert in it a recorded fifteen-second interview with one of the officers, and proceed to air the story on subsequent newscasts.

That night, you notice that your local newspaper carries the story about the accident, but the newspaper story is completely different from yours! In the first place, the names and ages of the accident victims are different. But you notice that the location of the accident as reported in the newspaper is the same location you reported in your story. Later that same evening, you receive a telephone call from a local citizen that sends you into mild shock. He states his name and says he heard you broadcast a news story earlier in the day that listed him as being killed in an automobile accident. You are stunned but admit that you did indeed broadcast such a story.

You decide then to retrace your actions over the past day to see how you gathered such inaccurate information. You discover that the people named in your story were not killed in the accident, but were actually involved in a minor accident that happened nearby. You remember noticing the sign post at the intersection where the fatality accident occurred and are sure you reported the correct location. You remember that when you asked the police officer for details at the scene, he walked over to one of his fellow officers and then returned before answering your questions. You recorded his statement, and included it in your newscast. You pick up the phone, call the officer you interviewed, and ask him about the mixup. He explains that he misunderstood your question. He thought you wanted to know about the minor accident nearby. He didn't know you were interested in the fatality accident, the details of which he simply did not have at the time. Embarrassed, you feel like not even going to work the next morning. Although all you did was try to collect accurate names, dates, and places, you failed miserably.

You can see how even an attempt to gather simple data presents difficulties. Obviously, the next time you are called to cover a similar story, you will make a second check. You might copy the names from the drivers' licenses of the victims and verify how old the victims are by checking the birthdate on their licenses. Or at least you might try to see the investigating officer's accident report. If neither of these are available, you could telephone the police station for details. After you jot them down, you could read them back to the desk sergeant to verify them. If you know, for example, that the accident occurred at 3:30 P.M., make sure the two of you are talking about the same accident. All of these *second checks* help to insure the accuracy of your story. They in no way guarantee it.

The above situation may seem rather simple. You think to yourself, the next time I'm assigned to a story, I'll do a better job of verifying the information. But will you? The next time such a situation occurs, you arrive at the scene of the accident and find two other competing radio reporters already there. Like you, each is equipped to broadcast live reports from their cars. You are the last to arrive, and they are already prepared to go on the air. You rush to the police officer, ask for the facts, and then prepare to report the story. Is it accurate? You really aren't sure. The other reporters have had the opportunity to check and verify the information. You haven't. Do you take the time to verify everything even though you will be scooped by your competition? Or do you air the story on the assumption that the officer is providing you with the correct facts, and it's time to report the news? As you head for the car telephone, you remember the voice of the man who called you the day you reported he was dead. You decide to let the other stations report the story. You'll wait and make sure the information you have is accurate.

These examples are typical of problems in achieving accuracy in radio journalism. First, although you presumed the police officer to be a reliable source, you found that under the stress conditions of an accident investigation, you couldn't rely on his being correct. He did not deliberately mislead you, but was simply preoccupied with the details of the accident and didn't hear your question correctly. Remember that information cannot always be received under optimum conditions, such as neatly typed press releases delivered to your office. Many times distractions come into play in the process of one person communicating with another. Coverage of civil disturbances, disasters, and other high tension situations involve pressures that can directly affect accuracy. This is especially true in radio journalism, where you usually need to gather facts and report a story within a relatively short period of time. Deadlines may be constantly less than thirty minutes away. Regardless of what time of day the story breaks, you have the responsibility to be on the alert for situations that affect the accuracy of news.

Dealing with the need for accuracy, Goodman and Perry outline the procedure to follow in broadcasting news of accidents:

1. Emphasize the source of the quote or information; plus
2. Give the exact location of the accident; plus
3. Give the full name of those involved in the accident; plus
4. Give the addresses whenever possible. (Don't forget that there are over a million "Mr. Joneses" and "Mr. Smiths" in existence and there could be more than one "William Jones" or "Tom Smith." An address helps positively identify the individual to whom reference has been made.)

The newsman must be extremely careful as to statements regarding cause and casualties of accidents and should never guess, but should he cite causes and casualty figures, *he must name his authority* as the information source to protect himself.[1]

Using Documents

Your experience with the fatality accident has taught you that people are not always the best source of accurate information. If you had checked the victims' driver's licenses and the accident investigation report, your story would have been accurate, assuming the licenses were authentic. Many times they are not if the victim is a fugitive with a criminal record. Had you looked at the accident report, the location of the accident would have told you that this was not the fatality accident you were reading about, but another one. In many cases where important facts are needed, a document—not a person—may be the safest assurance of accuracy. This is especially true when dealing with investigative reports with criminal or legal implications. When documents are not available, it may be necessary to contact more than one source to make sure that the facts are correct. Moreover, sources should be close to the heart of the information where they have direct access to information, not just second-hand assumptions.

Living with Competition

Competition can play an important role in the commitment to accuracy. Of course, competition among the press is basic in a democracy. Without it a free press would not exist. Radio journalists, with the means for instantaneous dissemination of news, are faced with an awesome responsibility to collect accurate information in relatively short periods of time and under the stress of competition. You can realize the frustration of being scooped by another radio station. But you can also realize that

[1] Jim Goodman and Larry Perry, in cooperation with Rudy Ennis, *Broadcast News And The Law* (Nashville, Tennessee: Associated Press State Bureau, 1973), p. 14. See also: *Perry's Broadcasting And The Law* (Knoxville, Tennessee: Perry Publications) 5, No. 20 (December 1, 1975), p. 4.

being accurate but last with a story is still more important than being first but wrong. Competition in radio journalism will be forever present in any community where there is more than one medium. In many markets, stations constantly stampede to see who can be first with the story. Thus, as a radio journalist, you will need to learn to work under the conditions of high-paced competition, accentuated by radio's frequent deadlines.

OBJECTIVITY

In the previous paragraphs, we have seen how difficult it is achieve accuracy, even in a simple attempt to report names of people involved in a fatality accident. Now add to the necessity to gain factual information the necessity to provide detailed analysis of a news event, and the problem of being objective becomes just as difficult as being accurate.

The pitfalls of objectivity can be illustrated in this relatively routine radio news story about the opening of a political headquarters in a small community:

LOCAL REPUBLICANS CELEBRATED THE GRAND OPENING OF THEIR PARTY HEADQUARTERS LAST NIGHT. EIGHTH DISTRICT REPUBLICAN CONGRESSMAN, JOHN SMITH, FLEW HERE FOR THE EVENING CELEBRATION AFTER SPENDING A BUSY WEEK IN WASHINGTON. EARLIER YESTERDAY, SMITH DELIVERED A MAJOR CONVOCATION ADDRESS AT THE UNIVERSITY AND ATTENDED A LUNCHEON IN HIS HONOR.

Let us assume you aired this story on an afternoon newscast. You were immediately contacted by the local chairperson of the Democratic Party, who took issue with the objectivity of your report. She complained that there was nothing "grand" about the opening of the local Republican head-quarters. She had driven by the headquarters at the time of the opening and had seen only a few spectators—she didn't consider that to be "grand." She also said that she knew for a fact that the congressman you said was "spending a busy week in Washington" had spent most of the week vacationing at his mountain cabin. She also noted that the luncheon following the congressman's address at the university convocation was not, in her opinion, held in the congressman's "honor."

As a reporter, you are somewhat mystified by the call from the Democratic chairperson. So once again, you begin to think back to how you gathered information for your story. You remember, for instance, that you had not been able to attend the opening in person, so you called the local Republican chairperson for information, knowing that he attended. You recall that he continually referred to the "grand" opening of the local headquarters and was very pleased with the attendance. You also remember that when you attempted to obtain an advance copy of Smith's convocation speech earlier in the week, his local assistant told you he didn't know if he could get you a copy, since it was difficult to reach Smith due to his many activities that week. Being unsuccessful in this attempt, you called the university to arrange an interview with Smith following his convocation address. The director of university convocations told you she wouldn't be able to schedule the interview, since the congressman would be going to the luncheon immediately following the address.

With this information, you composed your story about the opening of the local Republican headquarters. You never really thought about the adjectives you used. The local Republican chairperson was apparently not the most objective source to ask about the congressman's activities. You later confirm that Smith really did spend most of the week at his cabin in the mountains. You also realize that other important speakers had visited the university, and their speeches were normally followed by luncheons. You had assumed that because a politician was involved, the luncheon was in his honor. In the past you had covered many luncheons in Smith's honor, and without consciously thinking, you assumed this was a similar event. Obviously your story was not objective.

As a reporter, you must think carefully about the words you choose to write a story. Radio news copy is usually rather short. Every word carries an accentuated meaning. Since radio presents no opportunity to use pictures, words must tell the complete story. How would you determine what was a "grand" opening and what wasn't? By stopping to think, you could have corrected that mistake before making it. Never *assume* anything that you don't know for certain, such as the report about the congressman's busy week in Washington or how many people attended the opening.

To further understand objectivity, consider the example of what took place at a university one day when the president, learning of confrontations between police and students at a regional campus, called a meeting of local police and university administrators. The two groups met to discuss how police training would prevent overreaction by officers if trouble broke out on the main campus. The university notified the press of the meeting. The president figured that publicizing the meeting of police and administrators would alleviate any tension that might be developing.

Let us assume that you air a radio news story about the meeting. You are immediately called by the local president of the Fraternal Order of Police. He is upset because he claims you presented only one side of the story and, in his opinion, weren't very objective. The police official wants to know why you didn't interview leaders of campus protest groups to determine what those leaders could do to keep their followers from destroying property, thus necessitating police action. Once again you are mystified.

You had simply covered the meeting and reported it. It never occurred to you that even though the meeting in itself was important, perhaps it was only part of the story. You thought reporting that police and administrators had met was presenting both sides of the story, since they represented two different sides of the issue. Obviously you were wrong again.

So far, we have seen two examples in which news is readily available to the reporter. Next consider this situation: what happens when you must not only convey information but also analyze the situation? For example, if you are called to the scene of a civil war in Africa, you, as a correspondent, are responsible for reporting not only the actual statistics, such as the number of casualties or bombs dropped, but also for providing an analysis of the political situation that may have spurred the fighting. Certainly it is very difficult to be totally objective in this type of situation. No matter what viewpoint you represent, you may not be considered totally objective by any of the parties involved.

A similar situation could occur when reporting civil unrest. Reporting statistics such as crowd size at such events is only one part of the journalistic process. You also need to analyze the situation for your audience to help them understand why the event took place. When such analysis under the pressure of deadlines is part of the radio reporter's job, being objective becomes even more difficult.

You should remember that objectivity, like accuracy, is something very difficult to achieve. Although it is impossible to attain total objectivity, you do have the responsibility to always strive for it.

FAIRNESS

Interrelated with objectivity is fairness. But, whereas objectivity requires you to be free of emotion, fairness requires you to retain some sensitivity to emotion. Every time you present a radio newscast, your station's listeners await your judgment. Based on your judgment, they often make their own judgment about events and people in the news. For example, simply covering both sides of a political campaign cannot be considered fair if one side is given more coverage than the other, regardless of how objective that coverage might be. Neither could coverage of that same political campaign be considered fair if you were to cover one side of the campaign favorably and the opposite side negatively.

Fairness becomes a serious concern when covering such controversial subjects as race relations. You must ask yourself if the fact that an individual is a member of a minority group makes it necessary to report that fact. For example, is it fair in describing the accomplishments of an author for you to mention in the story that the author is black? Are you assuming, without justification, that this person is any more unusual because he or she is black, white, red, or yellow? Obviously it would not be fair to state in reporting a criminal action that an individual is of one race or ethnic origin, unless it had some direct bearing on the story. The exception is in broadcasting the description of a fugitive, although even this is open to discussion. The fact that a white man, a black man, and a Chicano clash in the street over an automobile accident is one thing, but to assume that the story necessitates mentioning that the individuals were Chicano and black and white goes beyond the role of an objective and fair report. On the other hand, if an American Indian was not permitted to join a fraternal organization because of his ethnic origin, then the fact that the individual was Indian would be an essential part of the story.

It is very easy to be unfair without realizing it. Stop and think about covering a political candidate who levels a series of charges against his or her opponent. As a reporter, are you obliged to be fair by providing the opponent an opportunity to reply to those charges? In the same sense, you ask yourself, should it always be one political candidate who is on the offensive and another on the defensive?

The sources used in gathering information also affect the fairness of your story. Consider, for example, that you are on the scene covering a story about amnesty for inmates involved in a prison riot. You decide to interview a prison guard to represent one viewpoint and a bystander to provide another viewpoint of the story. Would obtaining these two viewpoints be fair? The flaw in this method is that even though you have sources for different viewpoints, obviously the two sources' credibility and involvement with the issue are not equally valid. If the guard is opposed to amnesty for the prisoners, the fact that he is a guard gives his viewpoint credibility. But if your other source, the bystander, favors amnesty for the prisoners, what credibility does he have? One of your listeners could exclaim, "Well, I can certainly see why the guard doesn't want amnesty, but what does that bystander know about it? He probably has never been a victim of a serious crime." By using one credible source and one non-credible source, you are not being fair in your coverage. Much fairer treatment of the story could have been provided if you had interviewed a member of an organization working for prison reform.

It's not always the local radio reporter who is responsible for unfair news treatment. The radio news network can air a story that might upset the fairness balance of your station's news programming, For example, a member of a national organization recently chastized the U.S. Postal Service for very poor mail delivery. The remark was one-sided, and the radio news network carrying the story did not present any viewpoint from the postal service. Faced with a similar situation, you might follow up on the national story with reports on your local postal service. Perhaps your local post office is a national award-winner for efficiency and service. Yet your station, because of a broadcast over which you had no control, provided news coverage that was unfair to every employee of the local post office. An interview and audio actuality of your local postmaster's reactions to the national report would help in providing a complete, professional, and *fair* report on this issue.

Being fair is a goal that must be constantly pursued in good radio journalism. The rush of deadlines and frequency of newscasts make the goal difficult to achieve, yet you, as a radio journalist, must be sensitive to attaining this goal.

BALANCED BROADCAST

Along with the human element, the fairness and objectivity of radio journalism depend on unique technical factors—factors such as the positioning and distribution of stories. These elements are in many ways peculiar to the medium of radio.

Positioning of Stories

Scheduling a story as the lead (first) item in a newscast tends to give it greater clout than other stories in that newscast. To provide variety, radio requires considerable rewriting and re-ordering of news due to the large number of daily newscasts. The radio reporter would find it awkward to present fifteen hourly newscasts with the same lead story, unless some catastrophic event merited that story's continual lead position. This dilemma is unique to radio news; newspapers do not face it with their one edition per day; television stations do not face it with their three or four deadlines per day.

In the process of delivering up-to-the-minute newscasts, you as a radio reporter will most likely lead with one story at the 8:00 A.M. newscast and switch to another in the 9:00 A.M. newscast. In so doing, you must ask yourself if leading with one story and not another is fair to all of that day's "news makers." You must thus ask yourself, is this newscast balanced? This is not to suggest that you deliberately re-order news without any consideration for news value. However, on any one day, many stories have approximately the same news value, and re-ordering the lead story is not an abridgement of good journalistic judgment, but just the opposite.

Distribution

Distribution is another important aspect of balanced broadcasting. A story of greater news value, like the results of a Presidential election, will naturally be aired more frequently than a story of lesser news value, like the merger of two moderate-sized national companies. Thus, the number of times a story is repeated on the air (distributed) is based on its news value. But since many stories have approximately equal news value, you must guard against unconsciously providing considerably more exposure to one story than another.

Take, for example, the case of two political candidates. You may have covered their campaigns as objectively as you could. You may have included both positive and negative remarks from both candidates. You may have also included both offensive and defensive remarks of the candidates if they leveled charges against each other. Yet if you aired twice as many stories about one candidate as the other, you would not be presenting balanced broadcasts.

PERSONAL ETHICS

A radio journalist's personal ethics permeate every phase of the job. On or off the air, your life and actions continually reflect upon you, your station, and your profession. You must be aware of the effect of your off-the-air activities. Reporting radio news throws you into the limelight; you become a "public" person and are on display more than other members of your staff. Your voice becomes familiar to everyone, and everything about you, from your appearance to your language to your personal associations, directly reflects your integrity. Thus, moonlighting as a bartender at a dingy tavern might not help your image in the community or among your colleagues.

Political Activity

Your involvement in political activity may also reflect upon your work. Few reporters claim to be apolitical, but those who jump on a political bandwagon find it difficult to achieve objectivity and respect in their community. The news director of a local radio station who is also press secretary for the city's mayor may obviously seem biased to the listeners when he or she reports on the mayor's activities. Yet many radio reporters are involved in political campaigns, and some are even active candidates. This is fine if the reporter wins the election and then enters a political career. But if the reporter loses and returns to reporting news of the community, he or she may find it difficult to convince the public of personal objectivity in covering all sides of political issues.

We are not suggesting that you must isolate yourself from your community. In fact, later in this book, we discuss how active involvement in community organizations can help you as a reporter. However, if you become deeply involved in organizations associated with partisan politics or other political causes, you'll find it can have a direct effect on your job and your profession.

Accepting Freebies

You may also need to review your personal ethics when faced with the problem of receiving gratuities, or freebies, from people and organizations. For example, what do you do when the local Republican chairperson presents you with free season football tickets? Although you may be a great football fan, you may have to do some soul searching and ask yourself if you can be completely objective about this Republican chairperson and his party if you accept the tickets.

Some radio stations have a policy that prohibits reporters from accepting any gratuitous gifts or money, regardless of how small. Instead they allocate a budget for such situations as buying tickets for a reporter assigned to review a particular play. Other radio stations have no such policy, and the responsibility for accepting or rejecting gifts falls on the shoulders of the radio reporter.

Freebies present no easy answer. Some reporters feel that if you cannot accept small gifts without tainting your objectivity, then you really don't have what it takes to be a journalist in the first place. Others disagree totally with this viewpoint and say that you cannot accept one gift without accepting all others.

Let's examine the reporter's dilemma on freebies by looking at the case of a political party that schedules a $100-per-plate fund-raising dinner. A prestigious senator is going to deliver the keynote address, and you want to cover that speech. However, the party does not permit anyone to attend the dinner without a ticket. You have finally concluded that there is no way your press pass is going to admit you to the dinner, and you now have the choice of either accepting a free ticket or not covering the senator's speech. To add to your dilemma, your competition has decided to accept the free ticket and will provide full coverage of the senator's speech. Do you swallow your ethical pride and accept the ticket, or do you lose important news coverage? To complicate matters still further, do you pay the $100 and technically donate money to the party? Such a dilemma occurs frequently; you have to ask yourself just where you stand and where you draw the freebie line. No clear-cut answers leap out for this problem. When you are faced with it, you should at least stop to consider all the ramifications of accepting free gifts before you endanger your own objectivity. The issue of freebies demands that you be totally honest with yourself.

The Journalist As Mediator

Because of their familiarity to the public and their frequent appearance at the scene of events, radio journalists are sometimes placed in the position of *mediators* as well as disseminators of news. In certain situations, journalists are asked to go beyond their role of reporter and become actively involved in a news event. Radio journalists have been asked to mediate in disputes where hostages are involved or to broadcast exclusive information from an insurgent group. Such situations demand considerable thought. They demand decisions based on professional and situational ethics. If you were in this situation, you might ask yourself: "If I do become involved, can I report objectively?" "Am I being used?" Or, "If I don't become involved, am I endangering someone's life?" Perhaps you will never find yourself in such a precarious position, but the possibility does exist, and before it happens, you should at least ask yourself these difficult questions. The dilemma also has long range implications. As in the case of the reporter running for office, if you act as a mediator, will your listeners still consider you objective about the issue?

You may also have to ask yourself these questions in the face of competition. Assigned to a mobile news unit, you may find yourself arriving at the scene of a traumatic event before a local emergency unit does. Perhaps you arrive at the scene of an attempted suicide. The person about to jump from the top of a building is a personal friend. Do you get involved? While you're deliberating, the competing station is busily gathering information and recording an interview with an eyewitness. What do you do? Again, the answer is not easy, and every situation is different. But be aware that such situations can and do exist and that ethical and professional decisions must be made. It's sometimes helpful to consider these decisions in your own mind before you are actually faced with the dilemma.

Pressures from Management

One of the prominent citizens in your community whose firm is a major sponsor on your radio station has been arrested on a charge of drunk driving. The station manager learns of the incident, and before your newscast, calls to request that you do not air the story. You must make a decision. Do you air the story and risk angering the station manager and perhaps losing your job, or do you discard the story? No easy solution arises for this dilemma, either. Many radio station managers do not have a background in journalism. Also, their primary concern and responsibility is, and must be, for the profit column of the station. You, on the other hand, must live with your professional ethics and responsibilities as a journalist.

If situational ethics ever creep into broadcast journalism, it is in this area. Your best action would be to weigh the consequences. If you feel strongly enough about professional ethics, then you would air the story. However, regardless of how much you value your standards, is it fair to lose your job and make your family suffer the loss of income? When a situation like this does arise, it is best to consider its frequency and seriousness. If you are working for a manager who continually tells you what news to air and not to air, then you might consider seeking employment at another station. Notice we used the word "might." You must make that decision based on personal and professional goals as well as ethics.

In most instances, management will stay clear of decisions associated with reporting the news. This is wise, because for them to become too involved raises serious questions concerning freedom of the press. In other instances, a manager who has a background in broadcast journalism may like to maintain an association with the news department. When this happens, take advantage of his or her experience, but keep in mind that the ultimate responsibility for news judgment rests on your shoulders.

Taste

Recently a reporter asked the newly crowned Miss America, "How does it feel to be a piece of meat?"

Stop and think a minute. Is there a better way to ask this question? Do you or does management feel that you attract listeners by giving them a little sensationalism? Granted, public officials and public figures are in a position where every inch of their life may very likely be scrutinized by reporters. Some of the scrutiny is excellent; it usually separates the honest people from the dishonest ones. But do show a little sensitivity and tact. Intimate details about people's lives make news and give the public something to talk about, but they also focus an ugly spotlight on the journalist's lack of taste. That, too, gives the public something to talk about, and it gives journalists another obstacle to overcome in winning the public's belief and trust in news.

The Watergate era has generated a new dedication in reporters to search out truth. Unfortunately, it has also contributed to some reporters becoming cocky unprofessionals who make jackasses of themselves.

Ethics and responsibilities in reporting can lead a radio journalist into extremely difficult professional and personal decisions. Radio challenges the individual with its pressured pace of news deadlines, calling for the ability to make decisions rapidly and have those decisions reflect the positive aspects of ethics and responsibilities. No perfect answer exists for any of these dilemmas. As a human being, you can only strive to achieve the highest level of professionalism. This effort is a daily exercise in living and working, one in which time-tested experiences in different situations mold and direct you to a balance between your personal judgments and the ethical principles of your profession. That balance is usually precarious and constantly challenged. Yet awareness of some of the hurdles you may encounter in seeking that balance can prepare you to cross them with intelligent judgment and understanding.

SUMMARY

Like other journalists, radio journalists are entrusted with an awesome responsibility in gathering and disseminating news to the public. This responsibility is doubly awesome because radio journalists are subject to the constant pressure of frequent deadlines. Such responsibility demands total commitment to professionalism. One of the elements in this commitment is accuracy, an insistence upon carefully checking the facts. A second element, objectivity, entails the responsibility to seek and report all valid sides of an issue. The fairness element requires a sensitive commitment to "equal" reporting, so that the coverage given to one side of a controversy is relatively equal to the coverage given to the other. Another element is balance, dealing with technical aspects of radio news, such as the positioning of stories and how frequently they are aired. Finally, the commitment to professional radio journalism involves your own personal ethics that have a direct bearing on your profession.

SUGGESTED EXERCISES

1. Interview two radio journalists in your community and report on their stations' policy about freebies. Are there any exceptions to the policy?
2. Double checking news sources is one way to assure accuracy in reporting. List five other means you might use to increase your accuracy in reporting a story.
3. Assume that you obtain an audio actuality from your city's mayor about his views on a proposed city park. In order to broadcast an objective report, you decide to obtain viewpoints about the park from other concerned citizens. Select six citizens in your community that you feel would represent the viewpoints you need to present such an objective newscast.
4. You lead your newscast with the story about the proposed city park and include actualities of the viewpoints of concerned citizens. You first air comments favoring the new park, followed by comments against it.

Your news director tells you that this was not a balanced broadcast. Why would the news director have this opinion, and what could you do to improve the balance of your next newscast?

5. Suppose you are reporting a dispute over the granting of faculty tenure. One side in this dispute, the disgruntled faculty, is more than anxious to furnish you with comments and information. The other side, the university administration, is taking a "no comment" position. Would it be fair to air the comments of the disgruntled faculty, while reading the statement of "no comment" to represent the administration's side? Justify your answer.

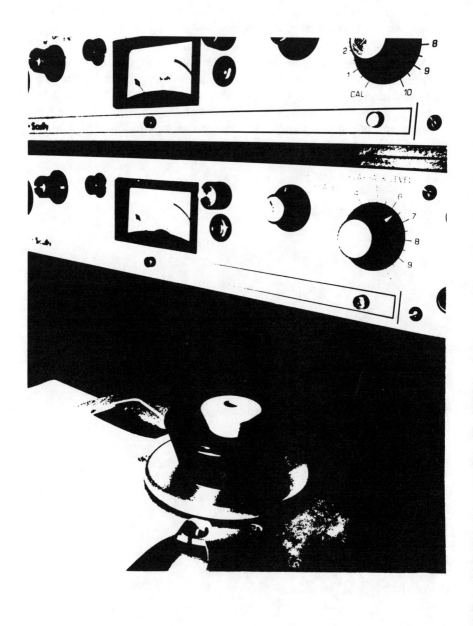

chapter three

News Sources

The comparative importance of news does not lend itself to tidy categories and automatic definitions. News judgment is learned over a period of time, tempered by ethics and refined by professional experience. News judgment is often indigenous to a specific community; what is news in one community may not be news in another. Similarly, one reporter's concept of news may be completely different from another's. You can become more aware of news sources if you first understand news types and news judgment.

NEWS TYPES AND NEWS JUDGMENT

In the course of their work, journalists have established certain basic categories of news, among them the concepts of hard news and human interest stories. *Hard news* is an integral part of any journalist's life. It refers to news about crime, major political or economic happenings, natural and civil disasters, and similar events. A radio station that emphasizes only hard news would report traffic fatalities, bank robberies, personal injury accidents, fires, candidates for major political offices, or announcements about plant layoffs. This news is relatively easy to determine. It makes up the daily logs of law enforcement agencies and emergency services. Even hard news will vary from community to community. A minor traffic accident that might make the evening radio newscast in a small community would be lost in the shuffle of fatal traffic accidents making the news on big metropolitan radio stations.

But even hard news has its variations, its angles, and its potential for another type of news—the *human interest* story. Take, for example, a story about a boy whose bicycle was stolen; he doesn't have the money to buy another one, yet he needs the bicycle for therapy because of a leg disease. Is this news? In most communities, bicycle thefts are not usually considered news. Yet there is a certain quality to this story that places it in a different perspective. It can become news.

Lost dogs in a town of one thousand people might be considered news. Yet in a major city, such reports would be impossible to include in the morning newscast. Consider, however, the story of a little girl who has lost the puppy her father gave her before he left for the war and was killed. That added element creates an entirely different news impact, and a reporter would probably consider this a legitimate news item.

Every retirement in a community obviously does not make the newscasts. Yet a story about a retired teacher reminiscing about her experiences during thirty years in the public schools would be of interest to every member of the community who ever sat in her classroom.

If we consider that basically news deals with events that affect people, we begin to see a foundation for news judgment. The examples of the lost puppy, the boy needing therapy, and the retired teacher would all be considered human interest stories. Like hard news, human interest stories are an integral part of radio journalism.

While keeping these news types in mind, remember that one of the most important qualities of radio news is *immediacy,* or when news happens. Radio has at its disposal the entire broadcasting day to disseminate news; it's not hampered by the evening paper deadline. Radio is *now,* and this quality of immediacy is inherent in radio as in no other medium.

Your understanding and awareness of the relationship between the types of news and their immediacy will help you develop a foundation for news judgment. The next step is to identify and develop actual sources of news. This is not an easy process. Some sources, such as the police blotter, are relatively accessible. Other sources for radio news develop only through weeks, months, and even years of personal contact with people. They result from creating a bond of trust and confidence. The following areas are a sample of the wide range of possible news sources available to the radio journalist.

GOVERNMENT

Government organization and action determine the laws and life of civilizations. More than any other institution in existence, it affects the daily lives of millions of people. It has done so throughout history and undoubtedly will continue to do so in the future. Government, therefore, consumes a great deal of the time and effort of any news-gathering organization as a source of interesting and informative stories.

Public officials constitute one of the most ample sources of news, primarily through the official duties entrusted to them by their electorate as mayor, governor, senator, or other public position. Your senator's vote on an energy bill or your mayor's action at a city council meeting are important news.

In addition to news about their official duties, information about their personal lives can also be newsworthy. If something in a public official's personal life is unusual or questionable, it can affect his or her official duties, and the public has a right to know about it. Laws have upheld journalists' rights to report the news of public officials' personal lives if such news is not presented with "actual malice"—knowledge that the news is false or reckless disregard of whether it is true or false.[1] For example, if a senator cheats on his income tax or remodels his home at taxpayers' expense, this is news. Other aspects of public officials' personal lives that become newsworthy include information on any of their financial dealings or holdings that may influence how they vote on bills or issues. Sometimes personal news can become very detailed, as in the case of Presidents. It's not unusual to report on a White House menu or what designer the First Lady employs to design her evening gowns. Harry Truman's homburg hat and John Kennedy's button-down collar set trends completely unrelated to any official Presidential directive.

Press releases from public officials can also be a source of news. Although you should be alert to their bias, public officials issue useful releases on a regular basis to radio stations on their mailing list. Some public officials mail certain releases only to certain media. Be sure to verify whether or not your radio station is included in *all* of these lists. You'll sometimes find that press releases scheduled for another medium or area can be an excellent source of news and might give you tips for additional stories.

Radio stations that employ and regularly schedule political analysts can totally monitor a political figure's life in order to give listeners the direct insights they seek. In some cases, a politician's written works are another important source of information. Books, articles, and monographs may provide insights not revealed in press releases, conferences, and daily interviews. If your local politician has written various articles or books, your news team and especially your station's political analyst should take the time to read them and, in some cases, reflect upon them on the air.

Political campaigns are also excellent sources of radio news. All political

[1] *New York Times Co.* v. *Sullivan,* 376 U.S. 245, 11 L. Ed. 2d 686, 84 S. Ct. 710 (1964).

activity accelerates during a campaign, exploding into a hectic pace of reporting speeches, covering meetings, attending press conferences, covering political rallies, and tabulating voter opinion polls. This frantic schedule holds true especially for radio reporters, whose hourly or half-hourly deadlines keep this type of journalist hopping.

With all of these considerations in mind, government provides one of the most fruitful sources for news. Because government affects all of us, it's the function of journalism to monitor it. For the radio journalist, this can be a twenty-four hour job. We'll examine political news coverage in greater detail in Chapter 4.

LAW ENFORCEMENT

Law enforcement is probably the single most common source of radio news for the local radio journalist. The "police beat" provides the journalist with stories possessing all the qualities we discussed: hard news, immediacy, and human interest. When crime or tragedy strikes, even though the number of people involved is small, the impact with which these people are affected is so great that it usually warrants news coverage. Covering law enforcement activities thus gives you access to much of the news that has a great effect on a community. In examining law enforcement as a source of radio news, it's important to know all of its branches and their relationships to the community.

The Police Blotter

The most common source of news in law enforcement is the police blotter, a daily log of activity that is common to all police departments. It's normally a sheet of paper with small paragraphs, each recording a specific police action and the time it occurred, such as traffic violations, arrests, complaint calls, and accidents. The police blotter is a public record. It customarily represents a composite of all uniformed police activity. As a radio journalist, you are usually the first reporter of the day to view the blotter. With many news deadlines facing you in a given day, you'll normally check it more than once.

Police blotters differ from city to city, depending upon what the police department feels should be made part of the public record. Some departments feel that openness is the best policy and place almost everything on the blotter; others leave out many activities that are legitimate news stories, forcing you to acquire the information through other sources. It can, however, contain items that tip you off to even more important news stories. Small communities may include activities on the police blotter that larger communities would not, such as reports of lost dogs or minor personal injury accidents. In large metropolitan areas, major crimes usually fill the police blotter, and minor police activities are consequently relegated to the department's telephone or radio log. In some communities, police officers are notorious for not updating the police blotter or for "accidentally" eliminating major items that might be of interest to reporters. Thus, although it is one source of news, it certainly cannot be the only source of news from law enforcement.

The police blotter, by its very nature, is designed for public consumption, especially by the press and public officials such as the mayor and his or her aides. Most of the information is in abbreviated form and might include these typical entries:

Monday 3/8/77

1350/ PI-X4, 10th & Greenbush, Invd. John Doe, 35, 223 Elm; Mary Doe, 43, 76 B Street; Damages: John Doe vehicle $400; Injury: Mary Doe taken to center Hospt. with lacerations. Investigated by 616, 775, and 334. John Doe charged with failure to yield.

1355/ Fire at 804 S. Pendleton. Arrested Josey Smith, 34, 66 Shady Apt. 4. Charged with Arson. Investigated by 545.

1500/ B&E, Ace Liquor Store. Subjects gained entry by breaking window. Stolen: 1 typewriter $400, five cases beer $40, handgun $100. Investigated by 775.

1530/ Fight at Pete's Joint. Arrested Hank Helpless, 45, 12 West Central. Charged with disorderly conduct, resisting arrest, assaulting a police officer, and DWI. Officer arrived to find Helpless had driven his car through the side of the tavern and was threatening the bartender, who wouldn't give him another drink. Helpless lodged in county jail. Damages: Tavern, $6,500; Vehicle totaled. Investigated by 616, 775, 334 and 714.

This sample police blotter shows it to be an obvious source of hard news. It also shows the necessity to understand the various police "codes" used to abbreviate information. For example, 1350 means 50 minutes after 13 hours, or 1:50 P.M. In our particular example, the symbol PI-X4 is a personal injury (PI) accident (X4). B & E is breaking and entering. DWI means driving while intoxicated. The numbers at the end of each entry after the words "Investigated by" are the officers' badge numbers. All police departments have different codes and terminology. Usually, departments will provide reporters with a key to the codes; if not, a few weeks monitoring police radios and working the police beat are all that's necessary to break the code.

The police blotter also provides material for radio news documentaries. For example, an entry about a child being struck by a car while bicycling to school can prompt your news team to produce a special documentary on bicycle safety, traffic safety, and school crosswalks.

Uniformed Officers

Uniformed police officers are privy to information you cannot receive from police monitors or police blotters. It is therefore essential for you to establish a good working relationship with these officers. Getting to know a police officer, however, can be a trying process. Like other people, police officers are human, and pestering them for news doesn't exactly make them feel friendly. But as a radio journalist, you need to gain information, and you normally need to gain it right at the time the uniformed officers are busy conducting a concentrated investigation.

In dealing with police officers, you must remember the rule of common sense. The pushy and demanding reporter who is continually provoking the local force will shortly find himself or herself cut off from information. This condition can become very acute in a small community. In some cases, one reporter on a news staff can make the going rough for all the others. But neither do you want to begin buying lunches in order to gain information. Some form of a mutual, congenial relationship between the press and the police needs to prevail if a free flow of information is to result. You must be prepared to report accurately, objectively, and fairly if your police source is ever involved in the news. Your source could be the victim of a police brutality suit, be censured by the department, or be part of a police corruption ring. This advice to be cordial but objective is applicable to other reporter/source relationships as well.

The Detective Division

The most "closed" division of the police department is the detective division, mainly because this division spends much of its time investgating, not arresting. Satisfactory relationships with detectives can be difficult to establish, since the radio reporter has the least contact with this type of police officer. In most cases, detective-related information only reaches the reporter after the arrest has been made. Nevertheless, knowing the detectives and learning about their activities can assist you in gaining access to information when it does become available. Knowledge about details of an investigation can help you predict when an arrest may be made, and that knowledge can often be the key to a major story.

Other Police News

The non-enforcement activities of the police department are also a major source of news. The alert reporter can note various activities in the policy and administration of the department and report these as legitimate news stories. These activities can include the promotion of officers, the appointment of new officials, the naming of citizen committees or review boards, the acceptance of local citizens for police recruit training, the planning of new safety campaigns, the training of school guards, and the inspection of motor vehicles. In some cases, state or city police departments issue regular press releases on promotions and other functions of their department. In areas where this communications effort doesn't occur, it is wise for you, as a radio reporter, to form contacts with the officials responsible for these activities. News of non-enforcement activities of the police department can often be a welcome alternative to a steady diet of police beat hard news.

The Element of Trust

Trust between people is universal, and it therefore applies to relationships between reporters and police officers. That trust may be tested at times when a law enforcement officer withholds information from a reporter. After all, the two forces involved are diametrically opposed to each other. The officer wants to withhold information, perhaps because of the secrecy of an investigation; the reporter wants to divulge the information in the professional role of news disseminator. At these times, the reporter will have to rely on conscience and common sense to make the right decision.

When you, as a radio journalist, receive confidential information with a request to keep it confidential for a certain period of time, you have the option of either releasing that information or withholding it. Releasing the information may instantly dry up your source; withholding it may be a disservice to your audience or give your competition the edge on the story. Because of the immediacy of radio news, radio reporters face this dilemma much more often than newspaper reporters. The newspaper reporter requested to withhold information at 9:00 A.M. isn't overly concerned, since the next edition won't hit the street until 4:00 P.M. However, the radio reporter requested to withhold information at 9:00 A.M. knows that he or she usually has the means to release that information at that very instant to the public.

Once more, common sense comes into play. If you value your source of information and have carefully established a mutual trust, you don't want to endanger this. Every officer, every reporter, every community, and every situation is different. Most police requests for withholding information come during major investigations or when a death occurs and the police department wants to first notify the next of kin before the news is disseminated. Departments differ on their procedure in these matters and some place the full responsibility on the reporter. The rationale for this decision is that police are in the business of enforcing the law and it's up to reporters to decide what information will be released to the public.

The relationship between reporters and police departments can range from hostility to mutual cooperation, with the norm being somewhere in between. This relationship, the key to one of the most important sources of news, is one that every radio reporter needs to nurture for the continued flow of information between the police and the press. You, as a radio reporter, must clearly communicate your need for immediate information to your local police officials. Many law enforcement officials are more accustomed to dealing with reporters from other mediums and don't understand why radio reporters are constantly checking with them for information. Once you do develop this understanding, your reporter/law enforcement relationship can be very beneficial.

THE COURTS

The judicial system has long been an excellent source of radio news. However, the broadcast reporter has encountered some frustrations tapping it. The broadcasting industry has tried to legitimize the use of tape recorders and television cameras in the court room with little success. Nevertheless, ample opportunity exists for stories to evolve from the court, and you should be alert to these. A view of the different levels of the court system provides a clearer understanding of what these sources are.

At the base of the court system is the *justice of the peace,* commonly called JP. With the exception of people wanting "quickie" marriages, the person who comes before the justice of the peace usually has been arrested for a traffic violation. Although this is not a source of major news, you should be familiar with the JPs in your community and call or see them when you can. Occasionally a prominent citizen may be brought before a justice of the peace, and such information can provide an interesting story. People charged with unusual violations may also be brought before the justice of the peace, such as the motorist caught driving 100 miles per hour in a school zone. A good relationship with JPs gives you access to these stories.

The jurisdiction of *city courts* is very similar to that of JPs; the distinction is a fine one and may differ from state to state. Certain city court cases may be continued beyond the normal one-day process or be bound over to higher courts, and this information can become news, especially if a prominent person is involved or a major crime has been committed. The astute radio reporter will keep track of various city court cases, especially those that are being continued. The very fact that a person does not come to trial until a year after being charged may in itself be a major news story.

At the county level are the *circuit courts,* which have a wider jurisdiction than JPs and city courts. In heavily populated areas where an overcrowded court schedule prevails, the circuit court may be made up of several divisions, such as probate courts or criminal courts. For the radio reporter, the circuit court provides an opportunity to cover a trial in considerable depth. Major trials in circuit courts can provide information for daily news coverage for two or three weeks.

The *court of appeals* and the *state supreme court* can also be important sources of news. These are higher courts that hear appeals from such lower courts as JPs, city, and circuit courts. Any time you cover a trial from your local community, you should be on the alert for a possible appeal. If a case is appealed, you should then follow up on the verdict of the appellate court, which will either uphold or reverse the lower court decision. It is important in covering higher court stories to include background information for those listeners who may not have heard about or have forgotten the details of the original case.

Federal courts decide on violations of federal law and major civil suits involving parties of different states. Just as other courts are fruitful areas for news, federal courts can offer significant cases too. Major crimes involving the transportation of material or people over state lines or investigations involving the FBI and federal officials usually culminate in federal court trials. Although the activity of federal courts may not be part of your daily newsbeat like the lower courts, monitoring that activity is still extremely important.

Cases before the *U.S. Supreme Court* are always of major importance. You don't have to live in or be part of the Washington, D.C. community to benefit from the Supreme Court as a source of news. Its cases deal with significant national concerns and usually develop from an appeal in the lower courts. In many cases, its rulings have a profound effect on local communities. For example, a Supreme Court ruling on the busing of school children affects communities nationwide. Thus, the Supreme Court becomes a news source for local stories with local reactions to the effects of national judicial decisions.

In some major cities, one radio reporter is assigned exclusively to cover the courts. That person is responsible for daily reports on judicial actions in the surrounding areas. This court reporter usually has some background in the legal system, either through education or experience. Such individuals can provide knowledgeable insights into the judicial process and can be a significant asset to their station. From their constant and concentrated coverage, these reporters are also able to mingle daily with clerks, judges, and attorneys, all excellent sources for radio news stories.

Continued efforts on the part of professional journalism societies and other interested groups may ultimately win permission for electronic equipment to be part of the American court scene. In selected areas, such breakthroughs have already taken place. As the courts themselves experiment with the use of videotape in recording testimony, the door may open, allowing other electronic equipment, namely audio tape recorders, to operate in courtrooms. When this does occur, it will present the opportunity to bring actual sounds of courtroom testimony into a listener's home, testimony which is on public record anyway. Should these new developments come to pass, a new era of broadcast journalism will evolve, and radio will have the opportunity to communicate this on a first-hand basis.

EDUCATION

Education affects everyone, either as taxpayers or as parents of school-age children. Since news of education affects the most prized possession of a family—the children—this news immediately captures the attention of listeners.

Education is a complex system. Because of its complexity, certain stations in major markets assign one competent reporter to cover educational news exclusively. The education reporter can become well known by school personnel and can become familiar with the intricacies of school board policy making. Like the court reporter, the education reporter can become a respected voice in the community who can set local ideas in motion by monitoring and reporting national trends in education.

Every activity within a school system is a potential source of radio news, regardless of whether it affects teachers, students, or administrators. Consider the student body, for instance. Many stories can evolve from this group: student government elections, science fair winners, a student amateur night, a class play, a volunteer class project for the orphans' home, a guest boa constrictor in a zoology class, the start of a student radio station, a fund-raising walk for muscular dystrophy, student reactions to open classrooms, or a scholarship competition. Student sports activities are also ample news sources. In order to keep abreast of this type of news, your station should subscribe to all of your community's school newspapers. Be they elementary, high school, or college papers, they are excellent sources of information to tip you off to stories or in-depth features about school activities. News about students, who are experiencing a most enjoyable time of life, provides a legitimate alternative and balance to the tragedy and bloodshed that are an inevitable part of radio news programming. But be cautious of campus news media. Where they lack responsible advisory supervision, they can be far less than accurate and objective disseminators of news.

Association with school administrators is important for a reporter because their policy-making decisions affect both children and parents. Any radio journalist should keep in close touch with school administrators at all times, for issues can develop quickly that necessitate a response from them. You should be able to contact school administrators at any hour of the day or night for their statements on such issues as school closings due to weather, or women athletes being prohibited from playing football.

School board metings are another source of news. Since they are so important to communities, some stations, with school board cooperation, broadcast the entire meeting live. This live broadcast usually stimulates new interest in the role and function of the community's educational system.

Don't forget teachers. Their activities are just as interesting to listeners as the news of students and administrators. Teachers' activities that can become radio news include special classes or seminars they attend to improve their performance in the classroom, teacher contract negotiations, summer activities, new teaching techniques, and the student activities they supervise. You may have assumed that news of teachers' activities would be interesting to the class but not to the public. Yet the public is interested in good teaching; after all, their children are vitally affected by it and their tax and tuition money pay for it. The radio reporter who calls attention to new and positive teaching techniques in a newscast not only provides a reward for the teacher who initiated those techniques, but also provides an incentive for other teachers to improve their own classroom procedures.

If a college or university is located in your community, this is an excellent source not only for news of that institution, but also for expert opinions about other phases of news coverage. The university's public information office can give you a list of faculty members to consult for comments about specific issues. For example, you could interview a nuclear physicist at the university on new developments in nuclear power plants, an economics professor on the decision of Congress to increase the national debt, a professor of medicine on experimental tissue used in plastic surgery, and an anthropology professor on the discovery of the remains of a prehistoric Indian village. You could also call on a broadcasting professor for comment on a new Federal Communications Commission regulation. Almost every news story has the potential for further analysis and comment by an authority in the field. Major colleges or universities can provide this information, which enhances the underestanding and coverage of events.

Education is life; we are constantly in a state of learning and, in a sense, of teaching. Education is a field from which springs research, technology, innovation, creation, and awareness. This field is vitally important to people, and people are vitally important to radio news.

BUSINESS

Many radio journalists tend to shy away from the business community, leaving those contacts to the sales department. Some reporters feel that publicizing business news implies prostitution of the news for sponsorship purposes. When this attitude prevails, the news team is actually excluding one of the community's major sources of news, one that concerns the majority of that station's listeners. The radio news team that covers business news professionally and completely can monitor the economic heartbeat of a community.

For example, let's consider the small business owner. He or she is concerned with making a living and a profit, and is always interested in knowing what other business people are doing. Such interest is the basis of discussion at country club functions and business lunches. After all, it's the business person's livelihood. A similar interest is found in the factory worker's concern about news of the factory or of the factory's products. You can build upon such interest in your newscasts.

Sometimes business news is concentrated in a separate news programming format, such as a business news final. This final can last from five to fifteen minutes and usually includes the latest stock market quotations. Such news as plant expansions, sales awards, new additions to a small business, new product lines, new franchises, management changeovers, and business consolidations are all of interest to the people of your community.

If your station does decide to air business news stories, you will find local business people more than happy to talk about their work. If your station decides not to air business news stories in regularly scheduled local newscasts, then think seriously about scheduling a separate business news program.

COMMUNITY ORGANIZATIONS

Some radio reporters make the mistake of excluding community organizations as legitimate news sources. This again is a mistake. Community organizations involve people, many people. News about these organizations and their activities concerns your listeners and deserves your attention, especially in small towns.

Hundreds of organizations function even in very small communities, and each of these organizations is a potential source of news. The Chamber of Commerce or the president of one of the service clubs may have a list of the organizations and officers in your community. If such a list has never been compiled, compose your own by calling officers of several organizations and have them refer you to officers in others until you create a working list.

Some community organizations are charitable, while others are primarily service clubs. Of the service clubs, the most common are Lions, Rotary, Kiwanis, Elks, the Shriners, League of Women Voters, Boy and Girl Scouts, and the Exchange Club.

Most of their officers are not skilled in public relations and are not used to receiving publicity for their activities. When they are approached, they're eager to enlighten you about their efforts. The market size of your station will determine how much publicity these organizations should receive. Obviously you can't report on the elections at every service club in a major city. Usually as market size decreases, the amount of radio news about community organizations increases.

At some radio stations, community organization news is relegated to a separate section of programming called the community calendar or community date book. When such a program exists, it is to your advantage to scan these news items. Obtain names of people to contact and start a file on community organizations to use as news sources. Especially in small markets, stories about activities on the community calendar are excellent sources for follow-up news features.

Some community organizations can provide an almost continuous source of news, as for example, United Way, the national service organization. United Way is fairly skilled in dealing with the news media, and its local director will either meet directly with media representatives or will appoint an information officer to handle publicity. United Way money-raising projects usually evolve over several months, and local business executives are "loaned" to the United Way during this period. Because of the nature and scope of their fund-raising project, United Way activities are a regular source of radio news for many consecutive weeks. Even when fund-raising is not active, stories about the upcoming drive and the people who will participate can add to your newscasts. Other fund-raising drives also make excellent sources for radio news, including muscular dystrophy walkathons, local Easter Seal campaigns, Red Cross blood drives, and the March of Dimes.

THE PROFESSIONS

We go to a doctor when we are sick, a lawyer when we need legal advice, and an accountant when we file our taxes; but you can count on one hand the number of times we consult these people as a source of news. The attorney is sometimes referred to casually for his or her role in a trial; the doctor is rarely mentioned, except perhaps in a malpractice suit; and the accountant is almost never mentioned. Yet, these professionals can provide a bountiful source of news for the inquisitive radio journalist.

Professional people should be contacted for the same reason faculty members are contacted—to provide local comments about issues in their area of expertise. For example, you may know the procedure for succession if the United States President dies, but what is the procedure if a county official dies? An excellent source for this story would be your county prosecutor. You could utilize comments from legal professionals on such issues as pretrial publicity, court trials of national significance, the importance of personal wills, the advantages of incorporating small family businesses, or citizens' rights to legal counsel. You might even weave a news or public affairs program around legal professionals.

The accountant is another untapped source for radio news. Remember, an accountant usually works for large corporations, auditing the books, advising on expenditures, and keeping an overall tabulation of the inflow and outflow of that corporation's cash. This work gives the accountant access to information about financial and business procedures. The accountant also prepares income tax returns, coordinates family financial planning, advises on acquiring property, and deals with other personal concerns. So, when major stories about court decisions affecting business clear your wire service, you would be wise to contact an accountant for clarification. The accountant can relate important national or state financial news items to local businesses, and you can air this explanation as a follow-up story or an in-depth analysis.

Local doctors and dentists can clarify developments in their profession in much the same way as accountants and lawyers can in theirs. For example, medical professionals are knowledgeable sources for stories on new drugs or on fluoride in the city water supply. An outbreak of a virulent disease in your community would be a reason to contact medical professionals for their comments. People are concerned about health care—their life depends upon it. Special radio news features on heart disease, vitamins, the value of exercise and diets, pre- and postnatal care, or mental retardation can be facilitated and heightened by expert opinions from medical professionals.

THE PUBLIC

The average citizen is a forgotten but extraordinarily interesting source for radio news. The primary reason is that the average citizen listening to your station can identify with the average citizen in the news. Your listener can say, "Yea, I know just what that guy's talking about." The average citizen also comprises the majority of your community's population and your station's listenership.

If you lose touch with the common people, you've really lost it as a journalist. They are closer to the heartbeat of your community than many political leaders. They have definite opinions although seldom express them; they want to take action but rarely do; they observe, contemplate, and sometimes stew inside because they have no outlet for their feelings. Many a successful radio personality has gained tremendous popularity and listeners by dealing with people on everything from talk shows to morning music formats, permitting them to call and express their views. As a radio journalist you should avoid limiting your contacts to community leaders, lest you forget what news is all about—the public. By mingling with people in supermarkets, gyms, department stores, churches, even bars, you'll touch the pulse of your community and the nation. It is also effective to give your listeners sounds of the public—extemporaneous comments and opinions that relate to every listener. Such topics as crime in the streets, food stamp programs, abortion, and the cost of living can all elicit lively responses from the public. The key is to obtain and air comments that present a balanced broadcast, as discussed in Chapter 2. Conservative, liberal, radical, Republican, Democrat or Independent—all sides must be represented. Once you meet this standard, the average citizen becomes a most abundant and direct source of radio news.

One further point. Certain stations that have a "talk show" or public opinion format feel this suffices to air the views of the average citizen, and decide that including these views in a radio newscast is therefore not necessary. Such is not always the case. Listen for about a week to a talk show and you'll find that, in most cases, the same individuals continually call in and are heard on the air. Others rarely express their views, so an opportunity for a cross section of the population to be represented in this type of programming is unlikely. If the radio news department accepts the responsibility to serve as an outlet for public opinion, a more accurate representation of public views can be presented to the listeners.

We've listed only a few of the almost infinite number of news sources available to the radio journalist. News is everywhere; it surrounds us. The astute reporter will look beyond the obvious—beyond the traffic fatalities, the murders, and the political gatherings—to a complete and total picture of the community. It is only by monitoring the pulse of the entire community that a station can effectively serve its listeners.

SUMMARY

News is happening all around you, and its sources are innumerable. One of the more important radio news sources is government and politics, whose public officials daily enact or reject decrees that affect the lives of millions of people. Law enforcement, from its gutsy police blotter information to its more discrete detective activities, is another vital source of radio news. Still another source is the courts, which encompass judicial actions at every level of society. The important activities of education, business, and community organizations provide the radio journalist with excellent sources of news. Professional people—doctors, lawyers, and accountants—are bountiful, virtually untapped news sources. The public, with all of its uniqueness, can be another unending source of radio news. This list by no means exhausts news source possibilities, for news surrounds you. It's up to you to decide where to find it.

SUGGESTED EXERCISES

1. Assume you are a reporter in a medium-sized market. From today's news, list five national stories that would prompt you to contact a local attorney for further insights into these events. Do the same for medical professionals and accountants.

2. Develop a list of major service clubs in your community and their officers.

3. Visit the local police department and ask to see the daily police log, or police blotter. Which entries would be legitimate stories for radio stations in your community?

4. Visit the public relations director of a college or university. Find out

what specific guidelines this person follows when dealing with the news media.

5. Visit five business people in your community and interview them about the activities of their corporation. List all of the possible stories that could result from your interviews.

chapter four

Covering Radio News

Covering radio news involves seeking out an event, examining it from all possible sides, and reporting these findings to your audience. This chapter examines some of the techniques to use in covering news as a radio journalist. It seeks to give you a head start. Let's begin with the interview.

CONDUCTING THE INTERVIEW

Conducting an interview is basic to radio journalism. In a sense, almost every contact you make creates an interview for the purpose of *gathering information*. Consider, for instance, your typical day on the job. It probably begins well before breakfast in contacts with the local sheriff, the state police desk sergeant, the city police officer, perhaps the front desk receptionist at the city hospital, and the fire department dispatcher. As you seek information from all of these contacts, you are interviewing them in the process. Beyond such routine morning contacts, later interviews are more formal and planned. The local senator may be in town for a luncheon, or a local business leader may announce plans for a plant expansion. Gathering information from these people may require in-depth interviews.

Radio interviews are unique, possessing qualities that distinguish them from interviews in other media. For instance, the radio interview is almost always recorded and aired verbatim, although perhaps in a shortened version. This means that the "uhs," "ands," "ers," and "hums" are all included, unlike newspaper quotations in which they are normally omitted. Sometimes so many of these utterances occur in an interview that it is impossible to air it. But on the other hand, if you do air it, you can often show the true reaction of an interviewee. Recording the interview also gives an exact record of what was said, so that the interviewee cannot charge that he or she has been misquoted; every sound and word is there.

Recording an interview does have its trying moments, however, and many a radio reporter has heard the phrase, "Let's record that over again," from interviewees dissatisfied wtih statements they have just made. Whether or not you rerecord is up to you. But the recording factor does create a unique relationship between the interviewer and the interviewee. Understanding the importance of stating an answer correctly the first time, the interviewee may answer your questions more deliberately and slowly than normal. If you ask a typical question, you may sometimes get a "canned" answer, since people who are interviewed frequently often prepare answers ahead of time, finding it easy to repeat them at every news conference.

An advantage the radio interview has over the television interview is that interviewees do not have television cameras and lights staring them in the face. Although most politicians and public figures are accustomed to this, average citizens are not, and it can make them visibly nervous.

Take the time whenever possible to thoroughly prepare your questions. Although some conditions, such as disasters and spot news coverage, do not permit this, other situations will. Scheduling a time suitable for both parties may seem obvious, but make sure you do it. And be punctual. If you're late, it can make both you and the interviewee tense and therefore not be conducive to a successful interview.

Putting your interviewee at ease is another important consideration. For some interviewees, seeing a reporter with a tape recorder has the same effect as a patient seeing a doctor with a hypodermic needle. When you sense that the interviewee is extremely tense, it helps to ease the situation by engaging in some unrelated and light discussion before you begin. Once you've started, asking some questions not directly related to the issue at hand can help ease the tension. But each interview presents a different situation. A politician interviewed about a scandal in the office projects greater apprehension than the local chairman of the United Way explaining this year's fund-raising activties.

The Telephone Interview

Many radio news interviews are conducted via the telephone. This is an advantage over television journalists, who must visit the interviewee in person if they wish to film or video-tape the interview. Radio's constant deadlines often force you to use the telephone. This eliminates a face-to-face confrontation, but it can come to an abrupt halt if the interviewee decides to hang up over a controversial question.

When you record a telephone interview, FCC regulations specify that you must inform your interviewee that you plan to broadcast the interview before you record it. A heavy fine from the FCC can await you and your station if you don't adhere to this rule.

The Crisis Interview

As a radio journalist, you'll conduct many interviews under crisis situations, such as natural or civil disasters, which will alter your interviewing techniques. You'll need to obtain specific information, your interview will usually be rather short, and the person you interview will normally be under great stress from the crisis.

Suppose, for example, you are sent to report conditions in a town just struck by a tornado. Unlike a normal interview, you can't expect to put a tornado victim at ease when he's just experienced the loss of his home. If you try to do so, the person may become emotional and refuse the interview. If he does consent to the interview, his answers may be incoherent; and although the interview may start, it may never reach a conclusion. Thus, the best approach is to be direct and ask only the necessary questions. Police officers or other officials may be equally difficult to interview when you're seeking answers about estimates of property damage or the number of people injured by the tornado. These interviews will also have to be rather short, usually lasting from one to two minutes maximum. Remember, people in crisis situations are under a great deal of stress. A prolonged interview won't provide additional information; it will only further upset people. Your job is to gather information and keep your cool.

The need for background information on the town and the people affected by a crisis usually develops within one or two days after the crisis has occurred. Your listeners know about the event; they now want to know how it affected people's lives. If you were unable to conduct interviews immediately after the tornado struck, you may be able to arrange them a few days later, after people have had a chance to adjust to the crisis. Then you can reap the excellent possibilities for stories on how emergency financial aid is being made available, how new living quarters are or are not being constructed, and countless other details about the post-crisis period.

Structuring Questions

The most important part of any interview is the questions. These are the keys which unlock the doors to information. If questions are asked improperly or if they are too complex, the answers will be difficult to use.

Basic rules exist for developing interview questions that you, as a radio reporter, can follow. These may vary according to the particular interview situation, but most of them have universal application to the process of one individual talking with another. You know that an exchange of information is going to take place. You want to gather information, but you also impart information in the form of questions. The key is to create an ongoing interaction between you and the interviewee so that you can obtain the maximum amount of information to use in your radio newscast.

Be direct and to the point. Don't ask general questions if you want specific answers. If you want to know how many people have been injured in a fire, don't ask a fire official, "What's happening?" The fire official might only give you a general answer and suggest that you ask someone else for additional information. If instead you had asked the official, "How many people have been hurt?" chances are you would have received your information.

Phrase your questions properly. The English language has rules of correct usage that apply to interviewing just as they do to writing. Improperly phrased questions are difficult to understand and may elicit completely different answers than you are seeking. Consider the interview with a local business executive whose company will begin manufacturing a new product. How would that person reply if you asked, "What are your workers' reactions in relation to this product?" This questions leaves more questions than answers. The executive may wonder if you want to know how the workers are going to react to additional employees being hired to manufacture the new product, or he may think you want to know if the workers are going to enjoy manufacturing this product in relation to other products they manufacture. But you may actually have meant to ask if the workers were going to buy the new product. All of these misunderstandings could have been avoided if you had phrased the question properly.

Don't ask double questions. Two questions expressed as one can cause a number of difficulties. First, it can create problems when you want to edit the answer to pertain to just one question. Separating the phrasing may be a difficult, if not an impossible, task. Second, by their nature, double questions tend to be complicated to answer and confusing to translate. Consider the following double question directed at a politician: "Why do you think Congress voted the way it did on this legislation, and what political forces will act upon local officials responsible for administering the funds?" This double question first forces the politician to provide a relationship between forces acting upon Congress and forces acting upon local officials. The forces may not even be interrelated. In addition, the answer to either part of the double question is a mammoth undertaking. No one likes to ask you to repeat the second part of a double question; that makes a person sound like a poor listener. On the other hand, in the process of answering the first part of a question, they may easily forget the second part. To compound this complexity, part of the interviewee's effort is spent remembering the second half of the question while he's answering the first part.

Don't ask questions with repetitive clauses. Say something once and stop; don't repeat the question, even if it's phrased differently. Consider the question: "Senator, could you explain by what process the Senate will consider the impeachment issue, and in what way will this body of government handle the case for the removal of the President from office?" The same question has just been asked twice. The reporter has forced the senator into an awkward position of either answering the question and stopping, thus seeming to ignore the second half of the question, or repeating the answer in a different manner. This awkwardness could have been avoided by a period after the word "issue."

Don't ask loaded questions. Questions with meanings already incorporated in them serve little purpose. You place the interviewee in a losing position no matter what he or she answers. Consider the classic loaded question, "Have you stopped beating your wife?" The interviewee can't win with such a question. It is easy for you to fall into this trap when dealing with controversial issues or with information you assume to be correct before you enter the interview. You may have heard that a senator is corrupt, so you ask that senator a loaded question about corruption, thereby giving him the choice of either admitting he is corrupt or not answering the question. Obviously, neither alternative is satisfactory.

Don't ask closed questions, especially if you want expanded information. By closed, we mean questions that elicit a "yes" or "no." If you're hoping for a reason *why* the congressman will or will not vote for the bill, then you've asked the wrong question.

The Element of Courtesy

Along with rules for asking good questions, elements of courtesy are also involved in a successful interview. Courtesy is a necessary prerequisite for satisfactory interpersonal communication in any situation. It's very easy to overlook many of these elements in the hurried pace of gathering news.

One of the first elements of courtesy is to *be a good listener.* Just as the people you're interviewing must listen to your questions, so you too must take the time and effort to listen to their answers. This is not only courtesy but common sense. By being an astute listener, you have the opportunity to expand your interview with additional questions. As a good listener, you can take advantage of a surprisingly effective interviewing technique—

silence. Interviewees normally dislike the awesome stillness between you and will often break these silences by giving you more information.

A second element of courtesy is to *give the person a chance to finish an answer*. Don't assume the end of an answer and ask another question before your intervieweee has completely finished talking. Obviously, two people can't talk at once, but many reporters try. Interrupting before a person finishes talking is an easy habit to adopt; since we're all receptive to non-verbal cues, we tend to interpret facial expressions or gestures and verbalize accordingly. This can create an overlap between your voice and the voice of the person you're interviewing. Once recorded, this overlap is impossible to erase. Broadcasting this overlap accentuates the rudeness, and that section of the interview must usually be discarded. In some cases, the interruption is not only rude but also tends to break the interviewee's train of thought, perhaps fostering a different answer than originally intended.

This brings us to another element of courtesy—*don't provide nonverbal cues*. Body language can be just as communicative as verbal language. When the interviewee is answering a question, don't provide nonverbal cues to elicit a response. Nodding your head is a common nonverbal cue. This action, although conveying approval of what a person is saying, is usually the reporter's nonverbal way to say, "Please keep talking" or "I understand." However, because head nodding does convey approval, the interviewee may note this "approval," appreciate the feedback he or she is receiving, and consequently respond more ardently than normal to a question. Although not consciously meaning to, you may be doing a disservice to your interviewee and your audience. Therefore, you must appear objective by avoiding any nonverbal reaction to the other person's comments.

An additional courtesy is to give the interviewee some eye contact. You don't have to stare him down, but you should at least look at the person while he or she is answering your questions. If you continue to gaze into space, a sharp, "Well what are you looking at?" may ruin your interview.

With these rules of technique and courtesy in mind, you can develop accurate and complete information by interviews. Even during crisis situations, you can give your listeners professional radio journalism.

THE PRESS CONFERENCE

If you were to ask most radio reporters their opinion of press conferences, they'd probably say there are too many of them. Press conferences are especially numerous during political campaigns or during the development of such issues as a new government policy or a scandal. Press conferences usually commence with a specific announcement from a "news maker," which is followed by questions from the press. "Press" can mean anywhere from two or three to twenty or thirty reporters, depending on how important the conference is and who's been invited. Exclusivity is nil at a press conference; any question you ask is public domain. But that means you also have access to information from other reporters' questions. This can be a major advantage of such collective questioning.

For radio, the key to a successful press conference is much the same as the successful interview. You must plan the questions you want to ask, since you'll be competing with other journalists who also want to ask questions. You need to realize that even though you're preparing questions, you may never have the opportunity to ask them. Time limitations force most press conferences to end before all of the reporters have had an opportunity to be recognized. Often the person holding the press conference has the option of recognizing only those reporters that he or she chooses. Many a politician has looked over a crowd of reporters, quickly spotting those who have put him in embarrassing positions in the past, and avoided recognizing them.

At small press conferences, reporters will often determine ahead of time who will ask the questions; in other cases, it's strictly a case of who can speak the quickest and the loudest. Competition among members of competing media abounds at a press conference. Stations want their reporters recognized as participants, and it's prestigious for the reporter to have his or her question and its answer recorded. Out of courtesy to all involved, no press conference should result in a shouting match. Most reporters realize that if they do not have an opportunity to ask a question at one press conference, there is always another. They're also quick to concede the floor to a persistent colleague, knowing that he or she very likely has a legitimate question which could benefit everyone.

Since press conferences can be lengthy, it's sometimes difficult to condense them into twenty seconds of audio actualities for a five minute newscast. Many radio reporters take along a note pad and jot down the tape recorder counter numbers that correspond to the place on the tape where important statements occur. This helps them quickly find those statements later when they prepare the newscast. We'll discuss the use of these audio actualities more thoroughly in Chapter 6.

Some press conferences are simply a ploy to gain publicity, especially when the news maker reads a statement and exits, leaving the press corps waiting. This type of press conference is a waste of the press' time and effort, since the information could have been communicated just as easily in a press release.

Press conferences can be terminated in one of three ways: The news maker can end it by excusing himself or herself and leaving. The news maker's aide can conclude the conference by predetermining the time for the conclusion; when that time is reached, the aide may close with, "Ladies and gentlemen, thank you very much." A third termination comes when the press corps simply runs out of questions, or when the senior member of the press corps present utilizes his or her right of protocol to end it.

Press conferences are a fact of the radio journalist's life and will continue to be a primary means of informing members of the news media about major events and opinions.

MEETINGS

Meetings, meetings, meetings! City council meetings, zoning board meetings, school board meetings, board of trustees meetings, public utility board meetings, county commissioner meetings, police merit board meetings—these are just a few of the public meetings covered by radio reporters. The task is to condense these meetings into a comprehensive, concise thirty-second report. When a meeting lasts as long as four hours, this tests a radio journalist's true ability. Some news formats permit longer coverage, depending on the size of the community, the importance of the story, and the length of the newscast. Some stations actually broadcast important meetings live in their entirety, although this is the exception rather than the rule. Even if your radio station broadcasts the entire meeting live, you will still be responsible for taking notes to use as highlights for later newscasts. Again, jot down your recorder's counter numbers whenever there is an important development so that you can quickly locate those portions of the tape to use as an actuality in your newscast.

If your radio station doesn't provide live coverage of major meetings, you still can use news and audio actualities of them. In this case you usually would not record the entire meeting when you need only key statements. But how do you know when to record and when not to? What if you miss something? These apprehensions can be partially overcome by obtaining an agenda of the meeting and checking those items that could develop into a news story. When such an item comes up for discussion, turn on your recorder. Again, it's easier to edit this information later if you note your recorder's counter numbers when important statements are made.

Unless a significant development takes place, coverage of a meeting will be written into a concise report, highlighting the major decisions and outcomes of the meeting. In a longer newscast, you might expand the story, highlighting testimony and including audio actualities.

Members of the audience can often give you essential comments about a meeting. Citizens groups appearing before a city council meeting, a parent-teacher meeting, or a school board meeting express opinions that may be important to a story. Recording such audience comments involves some ingenuity. You might enlist the help of a staff assistant who can sit in the audience with a microphone and a recorder. Special highly-directional microphones can pick up voices across rather large rooms. This procedure is necessary when microphones aren't furnished for members of the audience to voice their comments. It is also useful in recording speakers when you're not close to them or when desk microphones aren't hooked up to a central audio system.

SPEECHES

Covering a speech is much the same as covering a meeting. You'll primarily be reporting on what is said, recording key parts that represent the speaker's most important statements. Radio has an advantage over print journalism—it presents the actual sounds of the speaker's voice and even the audience reaction to them, instead of merely a printed text.

Electronic journalism has initiated another innovative form of news coverage called "instant analysis," which is commentary on a speech by two or three reporters immediately at the conclusion of the speech. These analyses are not as "instant" as they sound. Usually reporters have had an opportunity to review the text of the speech long before it's delivered. In fact, it would require immense professional skill for a radio commentator to provide an instant analysis *without* having first reviewed the text of the speech.

You'll need to follow some basic prerequisites in covering speeches. When possible, obtain an advance text of the speech and read or skim it ahead of time. Some speakers underline key sections of the text they feel are important; if a speaker has done this, take these notations under consideration, but also review the entire text on your own. An advanced text has a number of advantages. First it gives you a basis for forming questions to ask the speaker. Second, it clues you ahead of time when to record and when not to, saving considerable time and anxiety. Editing is thus simpler and quicker, since you edit while you record.

However, be alert to deviations from the text. Politicians are especially prone to this practice. Their speeches are usually written by professional speech writers, and they may either change the speech en route to the speaking engagement or extemporaneously discuss a late-breaking development in the course of the speech. If there's a radio reporters' rule of thumb for covering speeches, it's that any time the speaker deviates from the script, turn on your recorder. The deviation can be important, but it can catch many reporters off guard. A small innuendo, a side remark, or an off-the-cuff opinion can give a completely different meaning to the printed text. The alert radio journalist will be on guard for this type of diversion and be prepared to record whatever the speaker ad libs at any time during the speech.

Covering a speech may seem like a rather simple process, and it is, if you are satisfied to fall into the lazy trap of simply quoting or relaying the speaker's words. But speech analysis or rhetorical criticism is infinitely more involved, and the study of the process fills scores of volumes. You would be wise to read some books on the subject. They're available in most libraries and can sharpen your expertise in the reporting of speeches. Most journalists have never read a book on rhetorical criticism. This is disappointing, considering the frequency with which they are assigned to cover public speeches. By understanding some of the principles involved in rhetorical criticism and by utilizing the ability of the medium to provide the actual sounds of a speech, the reporter can provide a comprehensive, professional report.

LABOR DISPUTES

The American labor movement has found its way into almost every community, comprising, in some areas, the major part of the work force. Nationwide, union membership is in the multimillions, and organized labor has been established as a fundamental part of the American economic scene. It's a strong social and political force as well. You need to take stock of the role that organized labor plays in your community.

Organized labor uses the strike as a major lever in bargaining. When a strike occurs, you'll find yourself not only covering the strike itself but also reporting the impact the strike has on your community. Retail sales, bank loans, the depletion of savings accounts, and an upsurge in crime may all be related to a labor dispute and may warrant radio coverage. Radio is in a unique position to reach the labor union audience. Many factories or assembly line operations keep a radio turned on for the employees. As a result, union people often find radio their first source of news. This reliance on radio often gives radio reporters access to information about the strike not normally available to another medium. If union leaders know they can reach their members quickly via radio and want to make certain those members receive accurate information, they're willing to give that information to the radio reporter. Management also realizes this and can be receptive to radio reporters. The fact that radio airs the actual voices and thus lessens the chance of misquotes and distortion means a great deal to both management and union leaders.

Coverage of organized labor, however, should not begin at the time of the labor dispute. You should be aware of the length of union contracts, and note on your calendar the dates they expire. When the termination date approaches, check with union officials to determine what issues will be involved in the upcoming negotiations and provide coverage of those issues before the strike occurs, if it ever does. As with all news, it's imperative in covering labor issues that you be scrupulously accurate and objective in your reports and that you don't create undue alarm over the conflicts.

If a strike does break out, you'll be reporting both union and management's viewpoints and providing continuous information about the progress of negotiations. This will involve daily telephone or personal contacts with both groups. Obtain the telephone number and location of the place where these people are staying and contact them regularly.

During certain strikes, negotiations may take place outside your local community. When this happens, your station should make arrangements to receive daily reports, either by sending a reporter to that city to cover the negotiations or by hiring a correspondent or stringer to cover them. We'll discuss the role of correspondents and stringers in more detail in Chapter 5.

When the strike ends, radio is in a unique position to publicize it. For example, if a new contract is signed at 9:00 A.M. and the next work shift is to report to work at noon that same day, the fastest means of disseminating that news is through radio. Newspapers may not publish the story for another twenty-four hours.

Unfortunately, not all labor disputes are peaceful, and you'll need to be extremely cautious of news sources during times of high tension. Everyone will have an opinion, and distortion can abound. It's important to sift information for accuracy and verify it before you broadcast it. Distortion can only complicate the situation.

Covering labor disputes is a difficult and challenging process. Yet as a radio journalist, you have the means to gather and report news which has an instant and extensive impact on a community.

CIVIL UNREST

The civil rights demonstrations of the early 1960s and the campus unrest and anti-war demonstrations of the late 1960s presented a challenge never before experienced. Civil unrest was not new to the nation, but it was new to radio. The decade of the '60s thrust the radio journalist into a new role.

Covering civil unrest presents many problems which can be solved only by experience. Take, for example, the use of mobile news units. During the civil disturbances of the 1960s, many radio reporters found that these units and their live coverage capabilities were used by individuals or groups to gain media publicity for particular causes. Cries that the press actually caused civil unrest were heard everywhere. Radio had to take serious inventory of its coverage procedures.

To see why this inventory was necessary, let's look at the typical social structure of a college or university. Research has shown that the college student's major source of news is radio. Since there's usually not a television set in every dorm room or much free time to settle down to read newspapers, the student catches the latest news on the radio. Most college and university communities have at least one or two radio stations that reach the majority of the college listening audience. These stations can thus inform an entire college population about any activity taking place in the community and on campus. The civil unrest of the 1960s was a relatively new phenomenon to college students, something that to many was an "exciting lark." A live radio broadcast of a campus demonstration therefore became a magnet for other students, who came, not necessarily to take part in the demonstration, but to witness what was happening. What might have started as a demonstration of one hundred people often quickly numbered into the thousands due to continuous live broadcast coverage by a local radio station.

Every community has the potential for civil unrest. Recognizing this, you should familiarize yourself with issues in your community that could lead to unrest. The high tension atmosphere generated by civil protest is not conducive to objective reporting. The protest issues are usually polarized, and the information and opinions you obtain may represent the views of only a small group of people. The interviews you record may also be highly emotional. To read a statement by a protestor in an evening newspaper creates one kind of impression; to hear that same statement screamed into a microphone creates a completely different one. You must judge whether or not that impression is one that legitimately represents the majority of people present at a demonstration. You'll also have to take these same factors into consideration when interviewing law enforcement officers at the scene of a civil protest. Equally emotional and polarized information can come from this group. Again, you must ask yourself if those opinions are truly representative of what's actually happening. And when dealing with campus unrest, you must recognize that college public relations people will most likely not provide any more objective information than a police officer or a demonstrator.

This brings us to some specific reporting problems. For example, consider crowd size. In no way can you factually determine how many people at the scene of a civil disturbance are protestors and how many are bystanders. If you report that one thousand demonstrators are protesting at the courthouse and air the shrieking voice of a demonstrator, you'll give the impression to your listeners that a huge, berserk mob is about to invade the downtown area. Actually, most of those one thousand people may merely be onlookers listening to a vocal minority. Use caution when reporting civil unrest; make certain your facts are verified before you hastily and inadvertently alarm your community.

Thus, you have a four-way challenge on your shoulders: to be sure that your source is legitimately involved in the protest; to determine whether that person's comments represent the viewpoint of the entire demonstration; to obtain accurate, relatively objective information from officials; and to mesh this information carefully into an accurate, sane account of the situation.

Metropolitan radio journalists are relatively accustomed to reporting civil protest, but civil unrest can often develop in small towns where the local radio reporter is a neophyte to this type of coverage. In addition, small-town police departments may not be as extensively trained as those in larger cities and may be more prone to overreact to the protests. These two conditions can create a volatile situation that is a definite challenge for the press.

Distortion can easily occur in the process of news dissemination. The more people that information must pass through in the dissemination process, the more likely the chance for distortion. For example, you may write a news story about a local demonstration and give, or "feed", that story to a wire service. The wire service reporter who accepts your story may edit it. Then still another wire service reporter may edit it during a later shift. The revised wire service story may then be disseminated on a national basis and be picked up by a major radio news network reporter who further edits the story. By the time the story returns to the community where it originated, perhaps via the national radio news, it can be seriously distorted. The following example is an actual account of an occurrence during a campus demonstration.

On a major university campus early one morning, more than two hundred students were taken into custody by local campus police. They had been engaged in what the university president alleged was an unwarranted sit-in at a university building. Later that day, a group of approximately three hundred students occupied the halls of another university building. When they refused to leave after campus police ordered them to do so, the governor called in the highway patrol, who arrived on the scene approximately an hour later. In the meantime, all but about fifteen students had left the occupied building. The highway patrol, three abreast and eight deep, marched in a line to the occupied building. Approximately one thousand student onlookers stood outside and watched as the police officers entered the building. When the last police officer entered, some students refused to permit the doors of the building to be closed, and in an effort to shut the doors, the last police officer squirted a shot of mace at one student who was holding the door. The student let go of the door and it closed. Inside, the officer in charge spoke with the remaining students. No physical contact took place, and after a ten-minute discussion with the officer, the students left the building peacefully. The police officers then left the building, and the campus returned to normal.

The story was reported to the state wire service, which in turn edited the story. It was then used on the national wire, was picked up by a major network, and was subsequently used in a newscast by a local affiliate station of that network. A minimum of five, and perhaps many more, people had an opportunity to edit this story before the local station aired the newscast almost twenty-four hours later. Keep in mind the facts as stated in the previous paragraph, such as the one thousand students who were outside the building, fifteen students who remained inside the building, and that more than two hundred students had been taken into custody that morning.

The next morning, this is what the local affiliate station reported:

FOR THE THIRD TIME IN TWENTY-FOUR HOURS, STATE POLICE HAVE MACED ONE THOUSAND STUDENTS OUT OF A BUILDING AT THE UNIVERSITY.

In the actual story, the names and exact titles of the law enforcement agency and university were mentioned.

This documents how easily information can be distorted. In this instance, the various editing processes caused the distortion. The interesting feature was that the distorted report was heard in the community where the actual event took place.

Campus and civil rights protests are, for the time being, behind us. But civil protest is a very real part of American society. It can be found in a factory parking lot, on the steps of a courthouse, or in front of a government building. Since our Constitution permits and encourages freedom of expression and freedom of assembly, civil protest will always be with us. You, as a radio journalist, need to constantly be aware of the role your medium plays during these protests.

DISASTERS

Perhaps more than any other medium, radio truly serves its community during times of disasters. It is then that radio becomes the primary disseminator of information. It has the means to immediately warn listeners of an impending disaster and to broadcast emergency information to aid the disaster victims. It can disseminate news at a moment's notice from anywhere in the disaster area. When disasters occur, the transmitter radio becomes a lifeline for survival. In many communities where no television station exists, where the local newspaper is printed once a day or weekly, and where a civil defense warning system is non-existent, the local radio station is the *only* warning system available.

Other disasters may force radio into a role of restoring order to a community. A dam can flood an entire city within minutes, or a fire can quickly ravage multiple living units or downtown office buildings. The radio station will usually become a central information office, receiving and disseminating accurate information to the stricken community. During disasters, radio stations assume this role more than local police departments.

The best way to cover a disaster is to enact a plan of action long before the disaster occurs. The radio station should become integrated into the community's civil defense action plan or disaster drill. Your radio station's own disaster plan should delegate responsibilities but be flexible, for disasters can throw even the best-organized plan into disarray.

If your community is hit by a disaster, you should immediately assure your listeners that your station will gather and disseminate all information available. By doing this, you establish your station as a reliable, effective, and concerned source of information. Keep informing your listeners that periodic reports will be heard as soon as new information is known, even if you're providing continuous, live coverage of the disaster. This knowledge can provide stability and security for your community. Your station's news team should also repeat information on a regular, continuous basis during the disaster period. In this way, you're reaching those people who may have just tuned in. Listeners trying to obtain information about the fate of loved ones are not going to turn off their radio simply because they hear the same information twice.

Under a grant from the National Association of Broadcasters, Ohio State University professor James Harless and University of Oregon professor Galen Rarick, studied the operation of radio stations during three different types of natural disasters. Their research was summarized in ten guidelines stations should follow to provide news coverage of a natural disaster. These include:

1. A station should have a declared policy (in writing) for natural disaster coverage. Management should strive to incorporate the station disaster plan into the routine of the station, and practice it until all employees understand their roles.

2. Because there is sometimes little or no advance warning of disaster, emergency equipment should be kept in a state of readiness. Auxiliary power and transmitting equipment may be of great value when a natural disaster strikes.

3. The most vital service a station can offer during a disaster is thorough, factual news and information. Other programming is acceptable to the audience if it does not conflict with information needs. An overall, accurate picture of the disaster should be the goal of the news department.

4. Emergency transportation should be readily accessible. It is useful for covering the disaster and for getting otherwise stranded personnel to the station. Where it is not possible to purchase such equipment, stations might consider rental, lease, or other arrangements for the use of it.

5. Auxiliary groups or special clubs may provide valuable transportation and communication service if a station plans ahead with them.

6. Double-checking reports and "calling back" on volunteered information from the public should be standard operating procedure.

7. Personnel should not have to work to the point of exhaustion. Periodic rest and replacement should be included in the disaster coverage plan.

8. Telephone switchboards should be adequately staffed so that lines are not likely to be jammed and news personnel will not have to give all their time to handling calls. Preplanning for emergency communications and information channels with community authorities can result in the easing of telephone jamming.

9. The news department of the station has the responsibility of "watchdogging" the community disaster plan. Communities without disaster experience are particularly susceptible to confusion and disorder when a disaster strikes. In such a situation, the newsman finds it exceedingly difficult to meet his responsibilities.

10. Coverage of the disaster should not end with the "all clear signal." Intense reporting of available relief programs, investigation of the adequacy of the disaster response, of the aid programs for the victims, and of other "hard news" angles of the situation, are called for.[1]

Keep in mind that information may become emotionally charged and distorted during a disaster, giving birth to many rumors. Accurate radio news during a disaster is a very effective means of dispelling these rumors and holding panic and chaos at a minimum.

---

[1] James Harless and Galen Rarick, "The Radio Station and the Natural Disaster," Washington, D.C.: National Association of Broadcasters Research Report, 1973.

SPECIAL EVENTS

Special events occur in every community, and they're filled with human interest appeal. A county fair, an Easter egg hunt, a hospital dedication, a visiting dignitary, and the completion of a new civic auditorium all fall within the broad category of special events. The opportunities for developing stories around these events are numerous. Some of the following special events illustrate these possibilities.

Fairs

Almost every community can claim some form of celebration or fair as its own. These vary from the small agricultural fairs, such as the 4-H or Future Farmers of America exhibitions, to fairs featuring giant midways. Special fairs are sometimes held to raise funds for community organizations, such as hospital fairs and service club fairs. The importance of fairs from a reporting standpoint is that a large number of people participate in these events, and almost everyone, no matter what their age group, is interested in them.

Coverage of a fair should begin long before the event takes place. For example, many areas have fair planning boards that operate on a year-round basis. Others appoint a fair director who is responsible for the event's publicity. Although much of this publicity will be concentrated in the weeks immediately preceeding the fair, ample opportunity arises for news coverage during other times of the year. Special features on the role of these fair boards during the "off" season are excellent radio news copy, as is an interview with the fair director on his or her responsibilities. When a fair board signs a star attraction or finalizes a midway contract, when various exhibitors contract for fair booths—these are all of interest to your general audience. You can acquire this information through a quick telephone call to a fair board member or fair director. Since these people are usually accustomed to speaking to reporters, they can also give you informative statements to record and air as actualities in your newscasts.

The fair itself teems with opportunities for news coverage. The opening day gala often includes so many important dignitaries that your station could legitimately consider covering it live, or at least could employ on-the-scene reports. As the fair progresses, periodic reports from the fair grounds can provide additional news stories. Since most fairs revolve around various competitive events, the announcements of contest winners or recipients of prizes are cues for radio news coverage. Then consider the colorful happenings of a fair: a child reacting to a midway ride, a farmer discussing why his sow won a first place ribbon, a midway barker spieling his wares, a teenager explaining her entry in an art contest, and a grandmother reminiscing about the fairs of her youth. These are the stories filled with human interest, the stories that can make your newscasts vibrant.

Dedications

Dedications abound in every community: new shopping centers, new hospitals, new city halls, and new parks all prompt a dedication. These events usually feature well-known personalities or politicians, lending themselves to excellent news coverage. Your radio station may either want to broadcast the dedication live via remote equipment or record the ceremonies for later newscasts. While these celebrities are on hand for the dedication, take advantage of that fact and interview them, not only about the dedication but also on other unrelated issues. If a United States senator arrives to dedicate your city's new federal building, this is a perfect opportunity to interview her about a new Senate bill she's sponsoring.

When you're reporting on dedication ceremonies, you may also need to provide background information for your listeners, such as why the new building was needed, how long the new hospital has been planned, who donated the land for the new civic auditorium, and in whose memory the new park is commemorated. You can follow background information with supplementary stories, such as the advantages of the new sports arena for the community or the number of new jobs that a new plant will provide. By rotating all of these stories on various newscasts throughout the day, you'll give variety to your news and comprehensive information to your listeners. You can provide still more variety by rotating the actual sounds of the event, the actualities. For example, on one newscast you might air an actuality of the dedication, read your story about the effect the new building will have on the community, and read additional remarks from the speech of the presiding celebrity. On a succeeding newscast, you might air an actuality of the celebrity's remarks.

The amount of coverage you give to a dedication depends on the size of your station's market. Obviously, a metropolitan radio station in Los Angeles wouldn't have any air time left if it covered every new store or shopping center dedication. Yet in a small community, residents would consider such a dedication a major event. You, as a radio reporter, need to determine how much emphasis you and your listeners place on dedications and cover them accordingly.

Dinners

From the chamber of commerce, to the local utility, to a press club, to a service club—the dinners these organizations schedule fill many a reporter's notebook. However, some radio reporters tend to overlook these dinners as legitimate news events. Their preoccupation with politics and crime sometimes leads them to resist such "ordinary" happenings.

In smaller communities, such dinners are excellent opportunities to exercise some interesting radio journalism. In most cases, the dinner is called for a special purpose, such as a fund-raising campaign. A keynote speaker will most likely deliver an address at the dinner. Coverage of both the dinner's special purpose and its keynote address provides radio news copy, as does coverage of guests' reactions to the dinner and the speaker. Normally, the best way to cover these events is to record an audio actuality of the keynote speaker and perhaps conduct a postdinner interview. This combination will give you a concise report.

Again, the news value of any dinner usually depends upon the size of your station's market. In small markets, covering these events is important; in larger markets, only major dinners, such as a political fund-raiser, warrant your coverage.

Parades

Children's laughter, a calliope's shrill, a band's snappy marching tune, and horses' clopping hoof-beats are all sounds that are part of a great national tradition—the parade. The next time you're watching a parade, close your eyes and listen to those sounds. A parade is not only a visual experience—it's also a distinct audio experience. You can use those sounds to advantage in radio news, breaking away from the traditional news format.

For instance, record these enjoyable sounds and air them as background while you broadcast a report describing some of the key facts of the parade, such as the number of participating floats or animals. Or simply let these sounds speak for themselves in your newscast. Live broadcasts from the scene of the parade can provide additional colorful reports, which can include an interview with a clown, a band leader's reaction to winning the band competition, or an antique automobile driver's description of her car. The reactions of children to their first sight of a clown are unforgettable experiences to share with your listeners.

Commencements

Let us suppose that you arrive at the station one Saturday morning to find an assignment sheet from your news director instructing you to cover the commencement exercises at the local university. An important speaker is to appear, the state's secretary of commerce. The note goes on to say that you should have little difficulty in handling the technical aspects of the assignment. The microphones on the podium are connected to a patch panel, and you can simply plug your tape recorder into one of the patch panel outlets and record the speech. With those instructions, you take your tape recorder, appear at the commencement, find the patch panel, connect your tape recorder, insert a long-playing tape, push the record button, and sit back to daydream through the exercises.

You return to the station later in the afternoon and choose two segments of the speech you feel are appropriate to air on the Saturday evening and Sunday morning newscasts. The two segments you select deal with comments by the secretary about the future prospects for success of the graduates:

Audio Actuality: YOU AS SENIORS HAVE AN OPPORTUNITY TO CARRY THE TORCH OF THIS SOCIETY FORWARD INTO A NEW GENERATION OF PROSPERITY, ONE WHICH WILL LEAD YOUR UNIVERSITY AND YOUR COMMUNITY TO GREATER HEIGHTS OF RECOGNITION AND UNDERSTANDING.

Having recorded this audio actuality and written the proper lead-ins for this platitude, you place the cartridge tapes with the actualities on the news director's desk and drive off to the beach for the rest of the afternoon. Just as you're nearing the beach, you turn on the car radio to the competing station's news. Its lead story begins:

Announcer: SECRETARY OF COMMERCE JOHN DOE ADDRESSED THE GRADUATING CLASS AT CENTRAL UNIVERSITY THIS AFTERNOON. HE DECLARED THE STATE'S ECONOMY IS IN SERIOUS TROUBLE.
Audio Actuality: THE STATE BUDGET THIS YEAR IS NEARING BANKRUPTCY. THE GOVERNOR HAS INFORMED ME THIS MORNING THAT HE IS CALLING AN EMERGENCY SESSION OF THE LEGISLATURE TO DEAL WITH THE NEED TO RAISE TAXES, BOTH CORPORATE AND SALES. IF APPROVED, THESE TAXES WILL BECOME EFFECTIVE WITHIN THE NEXT NINETY DAYS.
Announcer: OUR CORRESPONDENT AT THE STATE HOUSE WILL PROVIDE REPORTS ON THE DEVELOPMENT OF THIS EMERGENCY SESSION BEGINNING AT 9:00 A.M. MONDAY MORNING.

You're stunned and wonder where the competing station got that story. You're furious at your assumption that the secretary must have granted an exclusive news interview to your competitor.

Actually, you received the same story. However, since you assumed that the commencement speech would only deal with the accolades of ivory towers, you didn't pay close attention to it. Your competitor obviously did. This was just the beginning of your agony. At the next hour's fifteen minute newscast, you heard your competitor lead with:

Announcer: ATTENDANTS AT THE CENTRAL UNIVERSITY GRAD-UATION EXERCISES THIS AFTERNOON HEARD STATE SECRE-TARY OF COMMERCE JOHN DOE SAY THE STATE IS NEARING BANKRUPTCY. HE SAID THE GOVERNOR IS SCHEDULED TO CALL A MEETING OF LEGISLATIVE LEADERS MONDAY MORN-ING TO BEGIN PLANNING EMERGENCY MEASURES. ACCORD-ING TO DOE, IN THE NEXT NINETY DAYS, WE CAN EXPECT SALES AND CORPORATE TAXES TO INCREASE.
WE'LL PROVIDE COVERAGE OF THESE LEGISLATIVE SES-SIONS BEGINNING AT 9:00 A.M. MONDAY MORNING AND CONTINUE WITH SPECIAL REPORTS FROM THE STATE HOUSE WHENEVER NEW DEVELOPMENTS OCCUR.
NOT ALL OF TODAY'S ACTIVITIES AT CENTRAL UNIVER-SITY'S GRADUATION CENTERED UPON ECONOMIC PROBLEMS. THE GRADUATES WERE EXCITED ABOUT COMPLETING FOUR YEARS OF COLLEGE.

The announcer then proceeded to air fifteen seconds of very short audio actualities of graduates expressing their thoughts about having finished their college education. Following these, you heard:

Announcer: PARENTS OF GRADUATES ALSO EXPRESSED JOY AND IN SOME CASES RELIEF.

This was followed by a series of short audio actualities from parents.

The competing station understood what you didn't—that covering a commencement takes much more than just recording the commencement speech. The participants in such an event can be a gold mine of news just waiting to be prospected. The same applies to many other events that could be termed routine and typical. Remember, look below the surface of the event. It's a bonanza!

THE HUMAN INTEREST STORY

The reaction of parents and students at the graduation exercises is an example of a human interest story. Human interest stories can either de-velop as an aside to a more visible story, such as the commencement, or can be an entity in themselves. They are stories about people, their experiences, and their reactions to those experiences—stories full of emotion and empathy. A human interest story challenges a journalist to create this *link* of emotions and empathy between the news maker and the listener.

Radio can help you form this human interest link through the dimension of sound. With radio, you can convey a small girl's ecstasy when a police officer returns her lost puppy, or the babbles of happiness when an impoverished high school student is awarded a full college scholarship, or the tender reminiscences of an elderly woman on the occasion of her surprise 100th birthday party.

The secret of covering the human interest story is to keep your eyes and ears attuned to the richness of life. The possibilities for these stories are infinite. Consider the voices of two boys bragging how their fishing worm sale will reap them a fortune, the modest recollection of a skier telling how he overcame polio to go on and win the Olympic downhill slalom race, the elderly couple's fears over not being able to meet their soaring utility bill payments, an auto worker's reaction to being laid off his job, and a teenage girl's reactions to the latest fashion craze. The hard or police beat news is important, but the human interest story makes a meaningful contribution of its own.

POLITICAL CAMPAIGNS

Our system of representative government gives the American journalist an experience that many of his or her colleagues in other nations do not share—covering the political campaign. Political campaigns occur at every level of our political system, from the local town clerk to the United States President. They also encompass primary as well as general elections. The news media cover these political campaigns and assume responsibility for informing the public of candidates' qualifications, activities, issues, statements, speeches, and strategies.

The Candidates

You only need to look at an election ballot to see the large number of candidates running for office at any one time. County commissioners, school board members, town officials, and state and congressional candidates all vie to represent one local district. With this abundance of candidates, many reporters tend to overlook minor candidates and instead concentrate on major ones. This is detrimental to the public and candidates alike because a local candidate may not have the means or the knowledge to conduct mass media campaigns to inform the voters. It therefore becomes your responsibility to inform those voters. Radio as a medium is particularly negligent in this area, especially on small stations where one or two reporters comprise the entire news staff. Obviously, the duties of these reporters are considerable, and at election time they may find themselves relying on press releases and covering only major candidates. On the other hand, radio's ability to air a large number of daily newscasts puts it in an excellent position to provide coverage for all candidates— local, state, and national.

You'll need to know where candidates are at all times in order to elicit a statement from them within a moment's notice. Since radio is not limited to one or two news deadlines per day, airing such statements from candidates, no matter what time they may say them or from what city they may be speaking, takes advantage of your medium's full coverage potential.

The Issues

Analyzing the issues in a political campaign can be a difficult process: the predominant issues are easily recognizable; the false issues need closer scrutiny. False issues are those developed by a political candidate to gain publicity. It is therefore vital that you keep abreast of all of the issues, real or false, involved in a campaign. You can accomplish this by keeping track of candidates' press releases and, to some extent, statements published or broadcast by other media in your community. It is only through this total monitoring process that you can cover a campaign successfully.

Coverage Considerations

For comprehensive coverage of the stepped-up campaign season, your station should have a well-developed network of stringers, tipsters, and correspondents. (These supplementary reporters are discussed in more detail in Chapter 5.) Take, for example, a congressman who is running for reelection. Although your station's listeners may represent only a small portion of the congressman's total constituency, they still deserve all the information available about him. However, your station may not have the personnel to provide coverage of him wherever he campaigns. So when he speaks in other cities, your station can enlist the aid of reporters in those cities to cover the candidate and feed the information back to your station. Your station can reciprocate the favor when the candidate campaigns in your town. Political candidates are less likely to make conflicting remarks in different areas when they know the information will be disseminated throughout the district. This method of cooperative reporting enables you not only to monitor the issues, but also to cover the entire campaign and meet your news deadlines, all at the same time.

POLITICAL CONVENTIONS

Radio reporters working for major metropolitan stations are routinely assigned to cover political conventions, yet radio reporters in small communities are rarely offered the opportunity. If a political convention is within a day's driving distance of your station, seize the opportunity to report it. If you do, you'll find the following guidelines helpful.

Coverage Opportunities

When you're assigned to the convention, your first concern should be to conduct interviews and provide analysis of issues geared to your local community. Networks and wire services usually don't cover such stories, either because they may not be familiar with regional politics, or they may not have the time or personnel to cover them. Your interview with your community's convention delegate can provide great interest and insight to your listeners. Your listeners can relate much more to the opinions of a local delegate than to those of an unfamiliar national correspondent. On the same hand, your local delegate will normally be more receptive to you, a hometown reporter, than to a strange national reporter. The local delegate knows you'll be reporting to his or her constituency.

Second, covering a major political convention is your opportunity for an educational experience benefitting you, your station, and your public. Perhaps nowhere else are actual political forces as intensely visible and active as at a political convention. You can become aware of the political forces that act upon your local and state delegates and can later use this understanding to provide deeper and more accurate insights into future political issues and events. Covering a political convention is an opportunity for professional growth that will permit you to serve your public better.

Coverage Considerations

Network and wire service reporters normally have access to the electronic facilities in the convention press room. Although some conventions do provide press facilities for local reporters, more often they are left to fend for themselves. For radio, however, this does not cause serious problems. The nearest pay phone or even your hotel phone can become the link to your audience. Your job is to provide expanded information for these people. Let the networks and wire services worry about time constraints and deadlines while you concentrate on collecting interviews and information from local politicians. Then, at a prearranged time, you can feed all of this expanded information back to your station via telephone. The station staff can edit your correspondent material, incorporating your interviews into audio actualities. In this manner, your station not only obtains primary convention coverage from the networks and wire services, but also supplements it with your additional coverage. For example, your station's hourly network newscast might contain network coverage of the major events at the political convention. Immediately switching to the local newscast, your station's news team could air your correspondent reports and audio actualities from the convention. This combined coverage provides comprehensive information to your listeners and gives your station the maximum benefits of its own convention reporter.

To get the most out of your coverage of a political convention, it's best to plan ahead. If you've never covered a political convention before, you should visit your local library and research back issues of newspapers and magazines published during previous conventions, picking up ideas of what might take place at the convention and historical background to include in your reports. Another preplanning suggestion is to obtain a convention agenda in order to organize your time for covering major events. It's also wise to know or at least have met your local delegates prior to the convention and be certain they know you. This familiarity is especially important during the high tension activity of voting and considering new convention issues. The delegate is not about to let a stranger take up his or her valuable time with an interview during voting procedures.

On the convention floor, a small transistor radio is a valuable reporting tool. It lets you monitor national or state network coverage and stay abreast of the latest convention developments so that you can seek out your local delegates for additional information.

When your station sends another reporter with you to cover the convention, you'll need a set of walkie-talkies to keep you in continuous contact with one another. You can use professional quality equipment to do remote broadcasts, with a portable transmitter on the convention floor. A receiver hooked into a telephone line can relay this remote broadcast live, via telephone, back to the local station.

As in covering labor union negotiations, you should obtain a location and telephone number where you can reach your local delegates. This gives you access to them at any hour of the day. To be courteous, you should notify the delegates ahead of time that you may be contacting them in the wee hours of the morning in order to make your station's morning news deadlines.

By following these guidelines, local reporters assigned to cover political conventions can provide coverage which is just as interesting and informative to their local area as the network coverage is to the nation. It's a challenge you will find exciting and rewarding.

SUMMARY

Chapter 4 examined the various methods of covering selected news events. In conducting a radio news interview, for example, you should put the interviewee at ease, structure your questions correctly, and adhere to basic elements of courtesy. When covering a press conference, the key is flexibility, whether you are asking your questions amidst throngs of journalists or recording the answers amidst occasional publicity ploys. When covering a meeting, your task is to condense the massive amount of material into a concise story. Speeches require you to sift through and rhetorically analyze the key elements in a prepared text, being alert for any textual deviations. Covering labor disputes involves year-round alertness for potential troublesome labor issues and dedication to objective and fair reporting, should these issues erupt into disputes.

News events that call for objective, calm reporting are civil unrest and disasters. Such special events as fairs, dedications, dinners, parades, and commencements will also be part of your daily coverage schedule. The human interest story adds an interesting and personal note to your radio newscasts. Finally, political campaigns, with their candidates and promises, and political conventions, with their nominations and hoopla, warrant your full, professional coverage.

SUGGESTED EXERCISES

1. Following the suggested interviewing guidelines, interview a city police officer and a city government official about their likes and dislikes about participating in a radio news interview.

2. With a tape recorder, cover one of your school's or community's special events. Discuss the different approaches you might use to write a story about the event.

3. Cover your community's next city council meeting. Prepare three audio actualities from the comments you record at the meeting.

4. Create a comprehensive set of guidelines to aid a radio news department in covering disasters.

5. At your school's next convocation, cover the speaker's presentation. List three different approaches from which you might write a story about the speech.

chapter five

Gathering Radio News

Many different factors affect a radio station's ability to be a dominant news force in the community. One of the most important of these is the skill of gathering news consistently with accuracy and speed. Operating on a continuous basis, this gathering process can become a well-oiled machine that continually absorbs and transmits information. Chapter 5 explains some of the processes involved in gathering radio news.

THE NEWS DEPARTMENT STAFF

The old proverb, "A chain is only as strong as its weakest link," has direct application to radio journalism. In order to have a successful news operation, the news department must consist of individuals who are qualified and work together as a *team*. Whether it is a twenty-member news department or one person working with other station personnel, it must be a total, combined, enthusiastic unit.

Qualifications

Qualified personnel are critical to the news-gathering process. Radio journalists enter the profession from many different backgrounds and walks of life; thus their professional training will vary. Some have had considerable experience reporting for newspapers and television stations; others are recent college or university journalism graduates. Regardless of these varied backgrounds, certain qualifications enable a radio news team to work together effectively.

Attitude. One of the most important is a positive, cooperative attitude. This plays an even more important role in radio than it does in any other medium. Radio deadlines are constant and quick, and the attitude of all members of the news department determines whether or not the professional work of the station will survive this pressure. In many radio stations, the staff of the news department is small, and personality conflicts can undermine the entire organization. Thus, a radio journalist must have the ability to work well with others in high tension situations.

Enthusiasm. Another important quality is enthusiasm. Radio journalism is a way of life. News that breaks at midnight must be gathered, reported, and aired before the job is finished. Audio actualities must be prepared *now,* not the next day. A story cannot rest on the editor's desk until tomorrow morning, when you may be more alert and can conveniently finish it. Also, station managers have neither the personnel nor the time to constantly supervise a reporter, so you must be able to function on individual initiative. Many times enthusiasm is the vital quality that distinguishes the professional from the amateur.

Seriousness. You must also be serious about your work. Some people enter radio news from programming, production, or other areas. You need to realize that attitudes of the news department may differ from those of other station personnel. News is not entertainment; it is business. It's a devotion that demands concentration and steadfastness. The lackadaisical, relaxed style that permeates some entertainment functions of the medium does not have its rightful place in radio news. Unlike the disk jockey's shift, which may begin and end at a certain hour, the radio reporter's schedule is irregular and demanding. This schedule requires a serious attitude.

Experience. Some things are impossible to learn in a classroom or textbook. Experience can often be the only teacher. The neophyte thrust into covering a labor dispute won't do the job of the seasoned professional, regardless of how much education the neophyte may have. You grow with your profession, and years on the job cannot always be equated with years in school.

Education. The education demanded of the radio journalist depends on the type of work in which he or she will be involved. A basic liberal arts education provides an excellent foundation for radio journalism. On the other hand, when specialized reporting is necessary, expertise in specific fields will become important. Reporters specializing in business news should at least have a basic understanding of economics. Similarly, if your station reviews the opening of the summer stock theatre and you receive the assignment, you should spend time learning about dramatic arts; don't just assume that attending a few plays qualifies you to write the review. **Writing and announcing.** The ability to write and announce are two other important qualifications. This does not mean to imply that radio journalism is "show business" or that you need that "golden voice" before you can succeed in the profession. Being able to enunciate and articulate, however, is desirable. An individual who can write but is not as skillful in announcing can be valuable to the station in off-air positions. People who are skilled in news gathering and writing can become excellent investigative reporters and do considerable off-air research, in situations where the familiar voice of the on-air reporter would jeopardize the investigation.

Keeping informed. In order to provide capsuled information, you need an in-depth understanding of an enormous range of topics. You must read continually and widely. Obtain copies of one or more newspapers and read them from cover to cover every day. Subscribe to weekly and monthly news magazines to learn more detailed information about the events and subjects you'll be reporting. The latest best sellers as well as scholarly studies should be on your reading list. If you're a specialized reporter, you'll need to be an expert in your special area: the education reporter should read current books on education; business and financial reporters should read business and financial newspapers and related books. Only through such constant and kaleidoscopic homework can you expect to interpret today's complex events to your listeners.

Staff Size

News department size is determined by the size of the station's market, the budget, and the ability to locate and retain qualified personnel. It would be ideal if every radio news director could have an unlimited supply of top-notch reporters who could be called upon, at a moment's notice, to accomplish any reporting task. Such dreams are not reality. Many radio news departments consist of one person. Major departments, however, can number as high as fifty people.

Supplementing the Staff

A station can supplement its regular news department staff in a variety of ways to increase its ability to gather news.

Interns. One way, without spending a considerable amount of money, is to develop an internship program with a local high school or college. Most schools have a communication or journalism program, and instructors are usually receptive to a professional internship program for their qualified students. Internships vary from one student working full time for an entire semester, to three or four students working part time for a few weeks. The most satisfactory internship program is developed through mutual agreement between the station and the school. Salaries for interns range anywhere from receiving only academic credit to earning full wages.

The internship program gives the news department the opportunity to locate qualified people who may become full-time employees after graduation. Internships do, however, demand some supervisory time on the part of the news staff. In most cases, though, the time taken to teach a student basic tasks can reap many benefits. In addition, internships help your station's news identify with the student body. Word travels among students, and they know what radio station is involved with them and for them. Internships enable a station to have an employee "on the inside" of the school. Many schools, especially colleges and universities, tend to be closed to reporters, and the only access to information is through university public relations directors, who may be less than objective in their approach to news. When a station develops a student internship program, personnel and information become available simultaneously, and the news department and students both benefit.

Correspondents. Another way to increase the station's news staff is to employ correspondents in major cities, such as Washington, D.C., the state capital, or nearby cities of importance to your local area. However, having that type of correspondent exclusively on the station's payroll is a luxury afforded only to large metropolitan stations. A Washington correspondent is usually either employed by a major network, a group of interrelated stations like the Group W stations owned by the Westinghouse Corporation, or he or she may freelance reports to a series of individual subscribers.

The advantage of a correspondent is that you have direct, immediate access to information concerning your local community that's unavailable from other sources. For instance, the state capital correspondent, aware of a senate bill that will affect your city, can provide you with an exclusive interview with the bill's sponsor. These exclusive reports can give your station the edge over its competition. In addition, most correspondents are experienced reporters. They know how to cover Congress or the state legislature. They know where the stories are.

If your station wants to consider hiring a correspondent, it's wise to contact those who are already established. These reporters usually offer their services on a fee basis. Another arrangement is to find a station that is willing to develop a cooperative trade arrangement with your station. A station in the state capital may be interested in receiving news of your region; you, in turn, are interested in receiving news of the capital. If you have the opportunity to become part of these cooperative agreements, the benefits can be substantial. A daily long-distance telephone call can provide you with an up-to-date and accurate report on news pertaining to your local area. Another advantage lies in this cooperative agreement, especially with reporters in a capital city; although their services may not be of great value during an average news week, they can be indispensable when the state legislature is in session.

Remember, however, that the cooperative arrangement must be of mutual benefit to each station. If you work in a small radio market, you will need to become an expert regional reporter and develop a pool of stories of interest to the state capital station. Therefore, you must be on the alert for news beyond your local community in order to carry your share of the agreement.

Stringers. The difference between correspondents and stringers is that correspondents report for a station on a regular basis. The stringer reports for the station only when a major news event occurs in his or her designated locale. Good radio news departments have a well-established network of stringers throughout the station's coverage area. Stringers can be invaluable in covering town meetings in small communities bordering a metropolitan area. They can also notify you of serious accidents or disasters and can aid in giving a local perspective on their community's government and politics. Sometimes teachers can provide stories on developments at an outlying school system and can follow through with in-depth reports. Unlike correspondents, stringers are usually employed by only one station and are normally paid by the number of their news stories that are actually used on the air. Sample fees for stringers range from unpaid reports from cooperative citizens to set fees for qualified reporters.

A well-developed radio news-gathering operation establishes reliable stringers in many different areas of the community. This includes not only geographic areas but various economic and professional levels as well. In instances where they are skilled in writing or audio editing, stringers can be equipped with cassette tape recorders to provide the station with information and audio actualities.

The station must make sure the stringers understand the responsibilities associated with their job. Station news staffs can prudently work with their stringers explaining the type and format of information that is of interest to the station's listeners. The stringer can be an indispensable part of any radio news operation. A good network of stringers can supplement a small staff and give it the news-gathering capabilities of a much larger station.

Tipsters. A tipster does just as the title implies, "tips off" the station to news events. From that point on, the station assumes the responsibility for gathering the information and reporting it to the public. Tipsters' qualifications and training are not important since they don't gather information, but rather alert the radio reporter to a news event. Some stations go to great lengths to encourage tipster activity by providing cash prizes or certificates at the end of each week or month for the best news tip. Reliance on the tipster is most beneficial in markets where considerable competition exists between radio stations. In that atmosphere, encouraging tipsters can help a station gain the competitive edge.

Confidential sources. As an investigative radio journalist, you will have contact with some sources whose identity will remain confidential. Chapter 8 deals with legal relationships with confidential sources in its discussion of shield laws. However, it is important at this point to point out that legal safeguards are involved when you deal with confidential sources. You must also avoid the pitfall of being "used" by confidential sources simply to further their own ends.

All of the above-mentioned personnel—interns, correspondents, stringers, tipsters and confidential sources—can aid you in the news-gathering process. They are supplementary to the station's news department, yet are indispensable in providing a total news picture to a listening audience.

WIRE SERVICES

As noted in Chapter 1, United Press International, Reuters News Service, and Associated Press are the three primary wire services in the United States. The advantage of wire services is that they provide you with news of distant areas, news you might otherwise find extremely difficult to obtain. Wire services can also tip you off to stories in your own community and provide you with a pool of ideas from which stories can be developed. For example, the wire might carry a story on national health care. You could then follow up by interviewing local hospital officials, welfare workers, and medical personnel.

Selecting a Wire Service

The quality of wire services differs from region to region. Wire services are only as competent as their personnel, and one wire service may be excellent in one state, but leave much to be desired in another. We have watched wire services in different regions rise and fall in popularity and efficiency. Sometimes the wire service that is best is the one with the most subscribers, mainly because more subscribers feed more news back to the wire service bureau, which then sends it out to all other subscribers. You should make a good thorough assessment of the wire services in your area and determine which one would be the best source for news. Keep in mind that the wire service your competition subscribes to is not necessarily the best one for your station. Reporters from competing stations sometimes refuse to feed stories to the wire service because these stories tip off their local competition.

Wire service subscription rates vary as much as news quality does. Most rate structures are negotiated, and like any business, a radio news department must bargain for the best possible contract. Items you'll negotiate include paper and ribbon for the teletype machines, two expensive necessities; some contracts provide these, but others specify that the news department purchase them. The new teleprinters use special paper without ribbon, but the subscription fees are usually higher. Educational stations that broadcast only during the academic year can negotiate a shorter contract and not pay for the service during the summer. These stations may also receive a non-commercial discount.

Wire services usually have reputable correspondents whose reports can aid considerably in key areas of your news programming. Some may employ a business or political analyst of long-standing reputation in your state, the advantage of whose association with your station may be the decisive factor in which wire service you choose. Since one wire service can't be first all the time or have access to every story, subscribing to more than one wire service has its advantages where budgets permit.

Specialized Wire Services

In addition to the standard wire services, other wires offer specialized news such as stock market reports, weather, agricultural news, or timber harvest reports. Some specialized wires even offer feed and grain reports; turkey and chicken market prices; beef, hog, and sheep market reports; and special farm radio news.

These specialized wire services can be a big help if you have the audience and budget for them. A station in a predominantly agricultural region might find the farm reports essential; a city radio station might not. Conversely, a major metropolitan station might be able to justify the extra expense of a business news wire, whereas a small town station might not. The decision to subscribe to a specialized wire should be made only after a serious cost analysis. Sometimes the money spent for a specialized wire could be better spent subscribing to a second major wire service.

SYNDICATED NEWS

Some radio news comes "prepackaged"; all you have to do to use it is to pay a fee. Most of these packages are feature news, editorials, or discussion programs. Organizations, such as independent news services, or individuals, such as leading free-lance journalists, develop these news packages and distribute, or *syndicate,* them to radio stations. The fee may be a flat rate for all stations or may be based upon your station's advertising rate card.

Some syndicated news features are free; all you have to do is to get on a mailing list. Such news is really a form of audio press release. Organizations offering such free syndicated radio news include governmental agencies, businesses, trade associations, and politicians voicing their views to their home town constituencies. Strict FCC rules on the use of this material in newscasts will be discussed in Chapter 8.

PRESS RELEASES

Press releases can provide leads to stories in addition to being news themselves. Most press releases are mailed on a regular basis by government, education, business, and industry. They are usually prepared by public relations people and consequently provide only the sender's side of an issue. However, it is important to be on the mailing list of *every* institution in your area. If your station's coverage area reaches into another state, then be sure you're also on the mailing list for press releases from that state. When contacting a public relations person, find out if you receive *all* of their press releases; you may find that you are on the mailing list only for selected releases. For example, the public relations director of a nearby college may feel that only information about students in your area is of interest to your station. You may feel that all news from that particular college is of interest to your listeners, especially if your own community has a college or university. The faculty of your local college may be extremely interested in what's happening to faculty at the nearby school. Thus, you would want to receive every press release, not just some of them. As we noted when discussing government in Chapter 3, don't take it for granted that you are on a mailing list. Find out for sure. It's better than missing a major story.

A reporter is usually deluged daily with piles of press releases and may be tempted to throw some of them in the wastebasket without taking the time to open them. This is a bad habit that should be avoided. The time you throw one away is likely to be the time you'll miss the most important news story of the year and be scooped by your competition.

EQUIPMENT

To ensure that all news personnel operate at maximum efficiency, one of the first rules of radio news is to be adequately equipped.

Tape Recorders

Every member of the news team should be equipped with a portable cassette tape recorder. The type with automatic audio-leveling microphones is easiest to use. In high noise situations, such as interviewing a fire official at the scene of a fire or talking to an assembly line worker inside a production plant, this particular microphone permits the voice of the person being interviewed to be heard above the noise. When the person is not talking, the background sound can be heard. Thus, the audio level of the recording is always constant.

Electronic Monitors

It's imperative that the radio news team keeps informed of the activities of such local emergency organizations as law enforcement agencies, fire departments, ambulance crews, and civil defense agencies. The most economical and efficient way to do this is to equip the station and news team with electronic devices that monitor two-way radio frequencies used by these agencies. Citizen band monitors can also be helpful.

Station budgets permitting, each reporter should be equipped with a portable battery-operated electronic monitor. Ideally, other members of the staff should also be equipped with them. A radio account executive may spend only a short time listening to the monitor between appointments, but it could mean gaining a lead for a major story. In small staff operations, a station engineer equipped with an electronic monitor can be a tremendous help in the news-gathering process.

Modern electronic monitors called *scanners* are capable of monitoring as many as sixteen frequencies. The units work with one crystal per frequency, and the typical metropolitan radio station will load the sixteen frequencies with crystals to monitor the city fire department, city ambulance, police dispatcher, police car-to-car, civil defense rescue, and other emergency services. The monitors are transistorized, can be left on twenty-four hours a day, and require little maintenance. During scanning, a small red light for each frequency flashes one-by-one on the monitor as the scanning device passes over it. When a particular frequency is in use, the monitor locks in place at that frequency until the transmission is concluded. The monitors come in portable versions about the size of a multi-band transistor radio and are easily attached to the power supply of an automobile. They can also be carried into the home, office, or to the scene of an event, providing continuous information about a fire, air rescue mission, a police dragnet, crowd movements, or similar situations.

Police Teletypes

Police teletypes are another means of keeping track of law enforcement. In some cities, instead of a police blotter, the police department uses teletypes to relay information to the press. Police teletypes have both good and bad qualities. First, a teletype creates a "communication distance" between the radio reporter and the local police department. Second, it provides an opportunity for the police to entice reporters into the habit of relying on the teletype, and then placing on that teletype only information that the department feels should be disseminated. Teletypes are fine, but if distrust or suspicion exists between the press and the police, teletypes only polarize these feelings.

Where teleprinters are used to communicate between police headquarters and police cars, standard police monitors cannot receive this information. In still other cities, police "scrambler" transmitters are used to garble the transmission between police headquarters and cars, again requiring a special receiving unit. At some radio stations, an astute engineer might build or adapt a commercial scrambler to the station's monitoring equipment so that the local news team will be privy to information disseminated via either police teleprinters or scramblers. In such cases, it's a good idea to check regulations first.

Walkie-Talkies

Most news departments have at least one set of walkie-talkies. These devices are helpful when more than one reporter covers the same event, as with political conventions mentioned in Chapter 4. Communication between the two reporters can aid in verifying information and eliminating duplicate reports when the reporters cannot be in direct proximity and compare notes. Walkie-talkies can also be used as an auxiliary relay device should a reporter's tape recorder fail to operate. In such a case, one reporter can relay an interview to another via the walkie-talkie and the second reporter can then record the interview. The purchase of a fairly sophisticated walkie-talkie system equivalent to what police departments use is justified. Since inexpensive models lack broadcast quality and require considerable maintenance, you should definitely avoid them.

MOBILE NEWS UNITS

Radio has the ability to broadcast news live directly from the scene of an event. These remote broadcasts, commonly called *mobile news* reports, are an important part of any radio news format. Mobile news units, either well-equipped automobiles, planes, boats, helicopters, or even snowmobiles, are indispensable in gathering these reports.

Ideally, every radio reporter should be equipped with his or her own mobile news unit. Stations usually assign such units to reporters on a full-time basis, and they become their personal as well as their professional car. Most units are acquired through trade-out agreements with local car dealers; capital outlay is thus avoided because the station makes arrangements to trade advertising time for use of the unit.

The degree of luxury of these units depends upon the station's budget and the decision of management. Some things, however, are important when choosing a mobile news unit. Keep in mind that the unit is a constant visual display of your station and reflects the image of your news department. A dilapidated "clunker" does little to enhance the image of your news team. On the other hand, expensive luxury won't hide a station's inadequacies in reporting the news.

Equipping a mobile news unit again depends on the station's budget. However, certain equipment is basic. One essential device is a telephone or two-way radio that operates on a high frequency band assigned to your station. The two-way radio should have a power output of approximately 100 watts and be transistorized. Such units permit you to broadcast live reports almost anywhere in a major metropolitan area. Another important piece of equipment is the electronic monitor. Again, the multi-frequency scanner provides you with continuous monitoring of emergency services. Also necessary is an AM/FM radio, which enables you to listen to your station and take cues directly from the air. The studio announcer can thus introduce you, then switch to the mobile news unit. In the unit, you're monitoring the studio announcer and can transmit the live broadcast directly on cue and on the air via the two-way radio. A portable tape recorder is also essential. Some units are equipped so that the tape recorder can be plugged directly into the transmitting system. This permits direct transmission of recorded information back to the radio station, and can be used to broadcast audio actualities or interviews, which can later be edited.

Wireless microphones and a special relay at the mobile unit's two-way transmitter permit the reporter to walk away from the unit yet still be able to transmit live over the radio station's main transmitter. A switch on the wireless microphone activates a relay on the mobile unit's transmitter and sends the reporter's voice back to the station, where it is rebroadcast to the listener.

In addition to this basic equipment, we also recommend some auxiliary items. These include brightly colored rain gear with your station's call letters boldly labeled on it. This not only is appropriate for inclement weather, but is also beneficial when walking about in "restricted" areas. Emergency flares are also recommended. You'll often arrive at the scene of an event before the police, and red flares can spell the difference between traffic safety and becoming part of the accident. In wintry areas, shovels, chains, and other road gear are a necessity.

Mobile news units can make a big difference in your ability to gather news and gain the loyalty of a listening audience. They have the advantage of carrying the news room to almost any point in the listening area.

MONITORING OTHER MEDIA

No reporter likes to admit that competing media are sources of news. However, it's not always possible to keep abreast of everything that's happening, and some stories are bound to escape the scrutiny of the best reporters. Therefore, some form of systematic monitoring of competing media is helpful in gathering information. In no way whatsoever should this be used as a substitute for good investigative journalism. But it would be a narrow-minded reporter who never read an edition of the local newspaper, never listened to a competing radio station, or never watched the local television news.

One Midwest radio station noted for its award-winning news discovered that the special frequency it used to communicate with its news helicopter was closely monitored not only by competing radio stations, but also by local police. To test the extent of the monitoring, the station decided to "leak" a mock scoop. After carefully alluding to the time and place of a fictitious drug transfer over the special frequency, the helicopter swooped down at the appointed time to hover over the "leaked" location. When they turned on their search light against the black of night, what should appear in the beam but three competing radio stations' mobile news units and a city and state police car.

The process of continually monitoring competing media presents the danger of creating paranoia among the news team. It is impossible to be first with every story. Morever, one medium will cover many stories that competing media will not. Although a systematic monitoring procedure is appropriate, it must be kept in proper perspective.

USING CONTACT MAPS

All journalists must keep informed, but radio journalists must keep informed continuously and instantly. Other journalists meeting fewer deadlines per day can learn of a news event two or three hours after it takes place; this is not the case with radio. Radio must bring information accurately and immediately to the listening public. An old saying states that some people have a "nose for news." An experienced reporter knows such a sense exists, but also knows that it's not entirely based on intuition. It's based on the law of averages. For example, a reporter knows that prominent people live in every city who are involved in government, business, education, law enforcement, and civic activities—which in themselves are news-producing professions and organizations. Therefore he or she builds a well-organized, current and complete telephone directory from these and similar sources. But the telephone directory is not always the most efficient way to gather information.

An ideal supplement to the telephone directory is a *contact map* of your area. This is impractical for large metropolitan areas, but is effective in medium and small market stations. A contact map is a blown-up city map with important telephone numbers marked on it at key locations where major news events are likely to happen. For example, you know that accidents often occur at a local industrial plant. The telephone number of the plant's public relations director is in your telephone directory. However, it's extremely helpful in gathering news to jot down telephone numbers of pay phones around the plant site and place them on your contact map. Normally when news happens, pay phones in the area are answered by personnel or workers on the scene, and those individuals may be able to provide you with an eyewitness report. In addition, law enforcement officials keep traffic accident maps and can pinpoint the probability of accidents at any intersection in the city. Fire officials can also pinpoint troublesome areas for fires. Telephone numbers of people living or working near these locations make ideal numbers for the contact map. A diner or gas station located at a hazardous intersection is another ideal telephone number for your map.

An easy way to place these contact numbers on your map is to use small gummed labels with a telephone number and name on them. These can be changed neatly when a contact number is no longer operative. When news happens at a particular location, a quick call to the contact number can provide prompt eyewitness information. From the perceptions and reports of reliable contacts, your station's news-gathering function can receive a big boost.

SUMMARY

Many factors contribute to the effectiveness of the radio news staff. Whether they be regular employees, interns, correspondents, stringers, or tipsters, personnel must have an enthusiastic and responsible attitude toward their profession and operate as a team in their news-gathering efforts. Wire services can aid the staff by gathering news from distant areas or supplying ideas for localizing national and regional news stories. Syndicated news offers in-depth feature stories, editorials, and discussions with national news makers. Still another link in the news-gathering chain is the press release and its informative yet sometimes one-sided views. Your station's equipment, such as electric monitors, walkie-talkies, and mobile news units give you increased capabilities to gather news and enable you to broadcast live from the scene of an event. Reliable sources to call and a contact map also help you gather information accurately and swiftly.

SUGGESTED EXERCISES

1. Discover which of your local radio stations employ interns in their news department. Interview one of the station managers and determine why he or she chose to participate in an internship program and how their program operates.
2. Find out which radio stations in your community employ news correspondents, stringers, or tipsters. Where are they located and how often do they report?

3. What program would you devise to entice tipsters to work for your station? Justify your answer.
4. Develop a contact map for your city.
5. Conduct a poll of the radio stations in your community to determine which wire services they subscribe to and why.

chapter six

Writing and Production

Radio has a style all its own. Through the use of words and sounds, radio creates images in the mind of the listener. Behind these images is a production process through which the listener hears, understands, and interprets the news. This chapter deals with this production process as it applies to radio journalism.

WRITING FOR RADIO

Writing radio news necessitates envisioning in your own mind the images to be created in the listener's mind. From this concept of writing for the ear spring several unique writing techniques.

Story Length

Story length is a major difference between radio news copy and news copy written for other mass media. The typical radio newscast lasts from three to five minutes, with forty-five second "news capsules" becoming common on some contemporary stations. The ability to condense a vast amount of information into this short time period is an art and science unique to the radio journalist. Moreover, this information must be revised and rewritten many times every day. For the radio journalist, deadlines come in multiples of eight, twelve, and twenty-four. Offering news on the hour and half hour, a large station may air as many as forty-eight separate newscasts per day. Contrast this with a newspaper with its one deadline, or a television station with its two or three deadlines per day. It's easy to see why working in radio means frequent rewrites.

If we examine a newspaper story of national importance and compare it with a radio story about the same event, the difference between radio

Tornadoes Slam Nebraska, Kill 3

OMAHA, NEB. (AP)—National Guardsmen patroled 3,400 square blocks of Omaha today to prevent looting after tornadoes killed three persons, injured more than 100 and did millions of dollars of damage.

The National Weather Service said the three twisters that hit Omaha were among several that struck wide-spread areas of Northeast Nebraska yesterday, causing loss of livestock and substantial property damage in rural areas. No deaths were reported outside Omaha.

After surveying the damage in Omaha from a helicopter, Gov. J. James Exon said, "It's just devastating. I've lived in tornado country all my life and I've never seen anything comparable to this for property devastation. This is certainly the biggest loss in property damage that ever has hit Nebraska."

He said at least 500 homes were destroyed and at least 1,000 severely damaged.

Acting Douglas County Coroner James Keenan identified the dead as Margaret Burke, 86; Lloyd Kramer, about 40, and Pamela Myers, 23. All were believed from Omaha.

Police said Kramer died when the roof of a Northwest Omaha service station collapsed while he was standing on it watching an approaching tornado. Keenan said the Myers woman, a waitress, died when the restaurant in which she was working was struct by a tornado.

He said he did not know how the other victim died.

Storm sierens started wailing at 4:30 p.m. as a huge black cloud moved in over the city from the southwest, and the tornadoes soon touched down. Forty-five minutes later, the storm alert was over, but sections of this city of 350,000 were in shambles.

The two areas most severely damaged were a 300-square-block area in the southwest portion of the city and its southern suburbs and a 500-square-block area in Northwest Omaha.

In the southwest section, the major damage was between L and C streets from 84th west to 132nd. In the northwest section, damage was concentrated from Grover Street on the south to

Maple Street on the north for several blocks on either side of 72nd.

Some of the most severe damage occurred at the 848-unit Wentworth Apartments, the city's largest. About 70 percent of the complex, which houses about 1,800 persons in suburban Ralston on the city's southern edge, sustained severe damage.

One Wentworth resident, Army Capt. William Rollins, said, "I'm wiped out. Everything is smashed to smithereens.

Another resident, Beryle Scott, said she was in her office overlooking the complex when the twister struck the building housing her apartment.

She said her first thought was, "Oh, my God, my children!"

She said she rushed to her apartment and found her two children safe, though virtually all her possessions were lost and two cars were leaning into the living room.

Other major structures that received heavy damage included several other apartment complexes, the Ralston Bank, Westgate Elementary School, Lewis and Clark Junior High School, Creighton Prep High School, Temple Israel, the First Methodist Church, the Downtowner Motel, Bergan-Mercy Hospital and the Omaha Playhouse.

Mayor Edward Zorinsky slapped a curfew on the damaged area at 6:56 p.m. and said it would remain in effect for 72 hours.

Exon called out all Omaha-area Army and Air National Guardsmen and said, "I think the danger of looting is very serious and we'll keep them here as long as we need them."

He said he would ask President Ford to declare Omaha a disaster area, making victims eligible for low-cost Federal recovery loans.

In Saunders County, just west of the Omaha metropolitan area, farm buildings, a garage and a home were reported damaged near Colon.

A tornado destroyed a grain elevator, lumber yard, grocery store, gas station, city hall and storage buildings in Magnet, a community of 88 in Northeast Nebraska. It missed a school by 150 feet, officials said.

Also in Northeast Nebraska, at Pierce, a community of 1,360, police

said a twister struck a half-block area. Several homes received minor damage and trees and power lines were downed.

Tornadoes also were reported sighted in Sarpy County, Nehawka, Plattsmouth and Fremont in Southeast Nebraska and at Stanton, Osmond, Winside and Randolph in Northeast Nebraska.

C. A. Stanley, a Boulder, Colo., businessman who was a guest at the Downtowner, said, "I didn't take it too seriously. I stood on a porch talking to a man and watched it (a tornado) in the distance. I saw debris and boards flying in the air. I heard a roar and said, 'It looks like we are going to be hit.'

"I headed for the bathtub in his room. I lost track of him and said, 'Where are you?' He said, 'I'm right here beside you in the tub.'"

And while thousands in Omaha scurried for safety as the storm siren first sounded, some 8,600 persons at the Ak-Sar-Ben racetrack took shelter for only a brief time.

Two funnels were visible from the grandstand when the track announcer told patrons to take cover. The brief rush to cover caused a six-minute delay in the third race. The remainder of the day's program went on as scheduled.

Figure 6-A

and print journalism becomes immediately apparent. The story in Figure 6A of tornadoes striking a midwestern state cleared a national wire service for use by newspapers. The following radio story of the same event was aired on a national radio network as part of a three-minute newscast:

Network Reporter: PEOPLE IN OMAHA, NEBRASKA ARE TRYING TO PICK UP THE PIECES THIS MORNING. THREE TORNADOES TORE UP TWO DIFFERENT SECTIONS OF OMAHA YESTERDAY, 500 TO 700 HOMES TOTALLY DESTROYED, ANOTHER ONE-THOUSAND HOMES BADLY DAMAGED. THREE WERE KILLED BY THE TORNADOES IN OMAHA. THIS IS UPI WORLD NEWS.

Newspapers can use an expanded story with detailed information; radio must condense it. Yet this radio story still gives the basic facts. Although longer stories may be appropriate in longer newscasts, it's the three- to five-minute newscast every hour in every day that causes the critical writing demand.

Radio News Writing Style

Notice how often the word OMAHA was repeated in the radio story. Radio is a fleeting medium. A listener whose attention was attracted by the word TORNADOES may have been alarmed and not heard the first mention of the location; thus it was repeated three times in the story.

The number of homes destroyed, 500 and 700, was expressed in numerals, as opposed to the words ONE-THOUSAND. In writing radio news copy, a good rule of thumb is to write out numbers under 10 and use actual numbers between 10 and 999. It's also helpful to write out hundred, thousand, million, and billion. You'll then combine these into one-thousand, 21 hundred, and 14 million-500 thousand, to cite a few examples. This style helps you read these numbers correctly on the air. In addition, when you have a figure like 2,456,789, round this off to APPROXIMATELY TWO AND ONE-HALF MILLION. Listeners can't normally comprehend the exact number if they're not able to look at it.

When you're dealing with abbreviations, beware. Abbreviate only those words that are intended to be read as abbreviations, such as AFL-CIO, U-N, A-M, P-M, Y-W-C-A, and Y-M-C-A. The hyphens between these abbreviations signal the newscaster to pause at the individual letters. NATO, on the other hand, is an abbreviation that needs no hyphens because it is pronounced as a name. On the list of "don'ts" for abbreviations, don't abbreviate names of cities, counties, states, months, days of week, official titles, and address identifications, such as avenue, boulevard, and street. Remember, what you write is what the newscaster broadcasts. Whether you will be broadcasting the news or whether someone else will, your job in writing radio news is to make the broadcasting end of it much easier.

Broadcast writing style is different and should not be compared with styles used in the print media. For more information consult the sections on "Quotes and Identification" and "Introducing Names and Titles" that appear later in this chapter.

The Radio Headline

The radio headline plays a significant role in condensing radio news. It lasts a mere second yet serves two purposes. The first is to inform the listener of top stories in the news. The second is to grasp the listener's attention and hold it. Although these purposes are similar to those of newspaper headlines, the difference is that usually all the radio headlines are presented in a group before any of the radio stories. It's much like the table of contents of a book, enticing the reader to keep reading. A newspaper leaves little more than a split-second difference between the time readers spot the headline and the time they actually begin reading the story. In radio, where a commercial comes between the headlines and the news, there may be as much as a sixty-second lag between the moment when listeners hear the headlines and when they hear the story. The radio headline must therefore compensate for this lag. It must also compensate for the conversational tone of a radio newscast as compared to a newspaper story. You're telling a story in a radio broadcast. Therefore, it's sometimes best to headline with a *soft lead,* one which normally does not cram *all* of the essential facts into those first words, but rather establishes the tone or setting of the story.

Radio headlines can be longer than newspaper headlines. Observe in Figure 6B the example of a newspaper headline in which an automobile

Ford to close
all plants in July

Figure 6-B

factory closes its assembly plants. Now observe the radio headline for the same story:

THE FORD MOTOR COMPANY ANNOUNCED THAT ALL 64 OF ITS U.S. ASSEMBLY AND MANUFACTURING PLANTS WILL BE CLOSED IN JULY FOR TWO OR THREE WEEKS, FOR WORKER VACATIONS.

Notice the expanded length of the radio headline. It needed to impart more information than the newspaper headline. It also needed to hold the listener's attention long enough to withstand a sixty-second commercial.

The number of headlines that precede a newscast may vary from just one highlighting the lead story, to a group of headlines encompassing every story in the newscast. Sometimes the sequence of headlines varies between local and world or national news. Compare a headline from a radio network's world newscast with one from a station's local newscast. The network headline, by famous newscaster Lowell Thomas, reads:

Lowell Thomas: FROM MOSCOW AND THE SUEZ CANAL COMES TODAY'S NEWS. GOOD EVENING EVERYBODY, THIS IS LOWELL THOMAS FOR CBS NEWS.

The local station's newscast begins with the headline:

Local Reporter: THE TOP STORY OF THIS HOUR IS THE CAPTURE OF A PHILADELPHIA MAN WANTED IN CONNECTION WITH THE MURDER OF A BEN SALEM TOWNSHIP POLICEMAN. MORE NEWS IN A MOMENT.

Obviously, it would have sounded strange for the Philadelphia station to have said, FROM WALNUT STREET TO INDEPENDENCE SQUARE COMES TODAY'S NEWS. Thus, the type of newscast determines the type of headline. Although not always the case, geographical identifications are frequently used to headline world or national news. In local news, the emphasis is on details of the story.

When only a limited number of headlines are aired at the beginning of the newscast, and not all stories within the newscast have headlines, it's possible to use a headline within a story. In other words, the first lines of the story serve as the headline, usually a catchy phrase—a soft lead— to grasp the attention of the audience. Read the following two stories. Notice how each employs a headline (bold type) as the first line of the story.

Local Reporter: WEST SIDE RESIDENTS ARE IN CHAINS THIS MORNING. A LATE SPRING SNOW BLANKETED THE WEST SIDE OF THE CITY LAST NIGHT. THE REST OF TOWN WAS UNTOUCHED. TRAFFIC IS SNARLED IN MANY AREAS WEST OF THE INTERSTATE, AND MOTORISTS ARE CROWDING GAS STATIONS WANTING CHAINS ON THEIR CARS.

POLICE WILL GET NEW BULLETS. CHIEF MELVIN HALE SAID YESTERDAY A SPOT CHECK OF PRECINCTS FOUND SOME OF THE BULLETS POLICE ARE CARRYING ARE AS MUCH AS FIVE YEARS OLD. HALE SAID THERE IS SOME CHANCE THEY MIGHT NOT FIRE IF NEEDED. THUS, MONEY FOR NEW AMMUNITION WILL BE PART OF THE DEPARTMENT'S NEXT BUDGET REQUEST.

Notice that in each of the stories, the first sentence was used as a headline. Using headlines at the beginning of stories is also the practice in some larger cities where a number of reporters are heard on one station. In such cases, a reporter will headline the story, then give his or her name before completing the story. Thus, reporters Martin Casper and Betty Smith would begin stories with the following lead:

WEST SIDE RESIDENTS ARE IN CHAINS THIS MORNING. THIS IS MARTIN CASPER. A LATE SPRING SNOW BLANKETED . . .

Betty Smith reports her story by saying:

POLICE WILL GET NEW BULLETS. THIS IS BETTY SMITH. CHIEF MELVIN HALE SAID . . .

In announcing this type of headline, the reporter *pauses* slightly *longer* than a period would justify just before and after the sentence that includes his or her name. In other words, Melvin Casper would pause slightly longer after the word MORNING and the word CASPER. Similarly, Betty Smith would pause longer after the words BULLETS and SMITH.

The headlines explained here are but a sampling of the many possibilities used in radio journalism. Headlines and headline formats are determined by the style, image, and identity of a radio station. All are used to provide a short synopsis of the story and to inform and lure the listener to stay tuned and listen attentively.

Writing and Rewriting

Radio journalists must not only write, but they must also constantly rewrite. This stems from the fact that the number of newscasts is far greater in radio than in any other medium. As we noted earlier, some radio stations air as many as forty-eight newscasts per day. To avoid monotonous repetition, the need to rewrite is obvious.

The key in rewriting radio news is to grasp the essentials of the story and then rearrange or reword them, being sure to retain the story's accuracy. With some stories, this process necessitates a complete revision; in others, just a change of a few sentences. New information may have become available and has to be included. In certain stories, just changing or re-ordering the audio actualities will accomplish the rewrite.

Rewriting takes practice. Although basic reporting classes teach rewriting, such assignments are usually designed to develop a story into its final publishable form. But keep in mind that in radio it may be necessary to write a story in as many as six or more different forms and incorporate audio actualities as well.

Using the story of the spring snow, we will demonstrate how the rewrite process develops. First, with nothing more than the first sentence headline changed, alternative leads could read:

SPRING HAS STILL NOT ARRIVED IN THE CITY . . .

or

THE CITY IS STILL WAITING FOR SPRING . . .

or

THEY'RE IN CHAINS ON THE WEST SIDE . . .

Countless other versions could be equally acceptable. The actual text of the story can also be rewritten. Again, using the spring snow as an example, different versions might read:

WINTER IS NOT OVER. GAS STATIONS ON THE WEST SIDE ARE FILLED WITH MOTORISTS THIS MORNING. THEY WANT CHAINS ON THEIR CARS SO THEY CAN DRIVE ON ICY STREETS. A SPRING SNOW COVERED AREAS WEST OF THE INTERSTATE LAST NIGHT BUT LEFT THE REST OF TOWN UNTOUCHED.

Still another version of the story might read:

HAZARDOUS DRIVING AWAITS WEST SIDERS THIS MORNING. A SPRING SNOW COVERED THE TOWN WEST OF THE INTER-STATE LAST NIGHT. ROAD CREWS REPORT ICY STREETS IN MANY AREAS. ELSEWHERE IN THE CITY, THE STREETS ARE CLEAR.

Neither story altered the information that snow fell on the west side of the city last night, that driving was hazardous, nor that motorists needed chains on their cars. Once completed, these two rewrites could be rotated among different newscasts. Varying the actualities of the story could also aid this rewriting process, as we'll see later in this chapter.

Write Concisely

In radio journalism, time is valuable. A four-minute newscast may contain more than fifteen stories; thus every word must count. Learn to write concisely. Use simple words but ones that say exactly what you want to convey. A good example of key words and pitfalls common to broadcast news writing appears in the *UPI Broadcast Stylebook:*

HURRY or just plain GO, not always RUSH.
SEND something, don't always TRANSMIT or DISPATCH.
CALL a person, don't SUMMON him.
BUY something, rather than PURCHASE it.
LEAVE a place, not just DEPART or EVACUATE.
ACT, don't always TAKE ACTION.
TRY, instead of ATTEMPT.
ARREST, not always TAKE INTO CUSTODY.
SHOW, rather than DISPLAY or EXHIBIT.
GET, don't always OBTAIN.
DOCTOR, not always PHYSICIAN.
BREAK, instead of always FRACTURE.

You should avoid many other similar words and phrases. In general, news must be directed to a mass audience, not a group of intellectuals. Also, since radio is a direct and instant medium, the listener must understand immediately what a word means the first, and sometimes the only, time he or she hears it. Concise writing skill comes only with practice, but keep in mind the basic guidelines every time you compose a story. Then, take the time to reread it and ask yourself if you could substitute any simpler words to say it better and more directly.

The Concept of Immediacy

Notice also in our story about the spring snowfall that the words THIS MORNING were used. Radio is an instant news medium. Therefore, use the present tense in your stories whenever possible. The words THIS MORNING give the story the impact of being "new" and specific, not general (as would have been conveyed by the word TODAY).

The Wire Service Rewrite

As already noted, wire services are not all alike. Their staffs are often composed of both broadcast and newspaper journalists. Even though the services offer separate wires for use by newspapers and broadcast stations, it does not necessarily mean that the people writing stories for the broadcast wire are grounded in broadcast journalism, or vice versa. You may find many stories on the broadcast wire written in newspaper style.

You'll also want to localize some wire service stories. Since the audience of the wire service may be either an entire state or nation, the references may be general, such as the words, THROUGHOUT THE UNITED

STATES. A Dallas reporter might want to localize this story with the words, THROUGHOUT THE DALLAS AREA or HERE IN DALLAS AS ELSEWHERE.

The primary purpose of a wire service is to relay as much accurate information as possible to subscribers. As a result, the actual length of a wire service story often necessitates that you rewrite and condense it. Also, the pressure of deadlines is felt in wire services as everywhere else. In the rush of sending as much information as possible with speed and accuracy, writing style may be sacrificed. Moreover, it would be impossible for wire services to prepare stories in a style suited to every station. As a result, rewriting wire service copy is a routine task in the radio newsroom.

Incorporating Correspondent Reports

As discussed in Chapter 5, a correspondent is essentially a person who reports on a news event happening away from the station's immediate coverage area. Correspondents usually work for a group of stations. Their reports may vary from fifteen to forty-five seconds, with especially important stories running one minute. You can write a correspondent's report into a newscast several ways. The most common is a simple introduction, such as AND NOW TO WASHINGTON, or WITH THE DETAILS, HERE IS WAZY'S JANE DOE IN WASHINGTON. Simply providing a headline and then switching to the correspondent is also common. A typical example would be, THERE'S NEWS IN CONGRESS THIS MORNING AS THE BLACK WANUT DAM PROJECT GOES TO THE HOUSE APPROPRIATIONS COMMITTEE. At the end of the word COMMITTEE, the next voice is that of the Washington correspondent.

Most correspondents use a *tag* to end their stories. The most common tag is one that simply identifies the reporter's name and the location of the report, such as THIS IS JANE DOE IN WASHINGTON. This type of tag is commonly called a *vanilla tag* because it associates no hard identity between the station and the correspondent. The vanilla tag is used widely by audio services where the same correspondent's report is sent to a number of subscribing stations. A more direct tag is one that reads, THIS IS JANE DOE IN WASHINGTON FOR CBS NEWS or THIS IS JANE DOE IN WASHINGTON FOR WAZY NEWS. This tag identifies the report, the reporter, the location of the report, and usually the call letters of the radio station or network. Tags can be worded many ways. Most stations that regularly use correspondent reports settle on one common tag to retain the identity of the station.

Remember, writing good radio copy takes practice. The stylebooks of both AP and UPI are excellent reference sources for this practice. And always keep a recent dictionary handy, as well as a world atlas.

ACTUALITIES

Actualities are the "actual" sounds of news in the making. It is the skill-ful use of actualities that differentiates the professional radio journalist from the amateur.

Earlier in Chapter 1 you were introduced to some highlights in the history of radio journalism. These included the sounds of reporter Herb Morrison reacting to the Hindenberg disaster and King Edward VIII abdi-cating the throne of England for the woman he loved. These were actuali-ties. For the radio reporter, the actualities may be the sound of a local politician announcing his candidacy; a police officer being interviewed at the scene of an accident; a professor explaining a new invention; a child expressing excitement over winning an Easter egg hunt; a fire official ex-plaining the damage to a burning building above the roar of sirens; or a stunt pilot describing how she'll perform a barrel roll over the county fairgrounds. This is the excitement of the actuality, lending a new dimen-sion of realism to any radio newscast. A truly professional journalist must go beyond the studio, beyond the wire copy, and beyond the typewriter to provide this realism to a listening public.

Actualities are not to be mistaken for sensationalism. Used responsibly, actualities provide maximum truth and accuracy. A politician's written ex-planation of his views on a subject gain new meaning when the politician expresses them vocally, with his volume, pitch, and rate providing the total meaning for the listener.

Actualities are one of two types. One is the *audio actuality,* which is a prerecorded sound used in a newscast. Many reporters shorten this term into the single word, audio. For example, a radio reporter may record an interview with a local university professor about a new invention. The reporter then selects a fifteen-second portion of that interview to use in a newscast. That fifteen-second portion of the prerecorded interview is an audio actuality. On the other hand, assume a deadline is fast approaching and time has run out to prerecord the interview with the professor. Instead the reporter telephones the professor, asks her to stand by, and then mid-way through the newscast asks her a question about the invention. The professor answers the question, and her actual voice is heard "live" in the newscast. In this instance the voice of the professor would be an example of a *live actuality.* Most actualities are prerecorded, or audio actualities; however live actualities are commonly used with late-breaking stories.

Judging the Length

Actualities can vary in length, depending on the format, production needs, or news value of an item; different news formats may necessitate different uses of actualities. As we'll learn in Chapter 7, a contemporary news format, in which the newscast lasts only one or two minutes, compresses a large number of stories within a relatively short period of time. It would thus be impractical to use a one-minute actuality in that type of format. On the other hand, an all-news radio format could easily accommodate a longer actuality.

As a general rule, most audio actualities in radio news are between five and thirty seconds long. The average number of actualities varies from one to five per each minute of news. Much longer actualities can be included in a newscast when some form of intentional interruption is used. For instance, when the news maker is interviewed by a correspondent, the correspondent's questions may be included on the actuality. Use longer actualities sparingly, though, for an individual's attention span on radio is not as long as it is for newspapers or television. The medium is not designed for that purpose. The same voice heard for too long a period of time can lose the listener's attention.

Selecting the Actuality

A five- to fifteen-second actuality may be taken from a speech lasting one hour or longer. Does this capsuled version of a news event lose its real meaning? Absolutely not. The total amount of news and information on any given day is impossible for one person to consume. Broadcasting every speech of every politician would literally take more time than thousands of radio stations could provide. Thus, the skill and precision of the radio journalist must provide the listener with a condensed, manageable summary of the most important news. Radio news provides listeners with the maximum amount of information in the minimum amount of time.

To better understand how an audio actuality develops, let's look at a sample interview between a reporter and a public official. For the purpose of illustration, we'll assume the public official is the head of the Department of Transportation in the city where the spring snow occurred. Assume our reporter, Bill Smith, telephoned the public official, whom we'll name Robert Carson. The interview went like this:

Smith: Bob, What is your department doing to help the situation on the west side?

Carson: Well, it looks as though we're going to be somewhat restricted. We have a number of large trucks out, and we're salting the area beyond the Interstate, and we've got the two new plows handling the Main Street hill area. But you know the bad part about this whole mess is that we—wait a minute 'til I get the phone—okay, as I was saying, the mess we're in. You see, we have most of the road equipment in the shop at this time getting overhauled, and it's not ready to go. And the real hangup is our salt supply is very low at this time of year, and that has caused considerable problems, along with many of the trucks being in the garage. It all adds up to a real challenge for our department. We took two of the plows out to the west side, and we have men operating them to try to clear a path for the salt trucks, which have, by the way, the last two loads of salt in our stockpile, so it could be a problem later this morning if it keeps snowing. If we can just get a break in the weather, we'll have it licked. But hopefully, motorists who don't absolutely have to drive this morning will stay off the streets. This would be a tremendous help.

Smith: Okay, thanks Bob. I'll check back with you later.

Now Bill Smith wants to prepare a story using a portion of the prerecorded interview. After listening to the interview again, he prepares a set of actualities. He chooses four actualities, placing each actuality on a separate cartridge tape. The first is Carson's comments on where his department is working:

Carson: WE HAVE A NUMBER OF LARGE TRUCKS OUT, AND WE'RE SALTING THE AREA BEYOND THE INTERSTATE, AND WE'VE GOT THE TWO NEW PLOWS HANDLING THE MAIN STREET HILL AREA.

The second actuality, which Smith places on a separate cartridge tape, concerns the salt supply and the truck maintenance problems:

Carson: OUR SALT SUPPLY IS VERY LOW AT THIS TIME OF YEAR AND THAT HAS CAUSED CONSIDERABLE PROBLEMS, ALONG WITH MANY OF THE TRUCKS BEING IN THE GARAGE.

Still another actuality is placed on the third cartridge tape. This time Smith records Carson's second comment about the trucks and the salt supply:

Carson: WE TOOK TWO OF THE PLOWS OUT TO THE WEST SIDE, AND WE HAVE MEN OPERATING THEM TO TRY TO CLEAR A PATH FOR THE SALT TRUCKS, WHICH HAVE, BY THE WAY, THE LAST TWO LOADS OF SALT IN OUR STOCKPILE, SO IT COULD BE A PROBLEM LATER THIS MORNING IF IT KEEPS SNOWING.

Although that comment was one in which Carson basically repeated himself, Smith decides he will keep it because he can use it on a rotating basis in much the same way that a story rewrite would be rotated. Finally, Smith decides to produce an actuality from Carson's warning to motorists to stay off the road. Again on a separate cartridge tape, Smith records the comment:

Carson: HOPEFULLY, MOTORISTS WHO DON'T ABSOLUTELY HAVE TO DRIVE THIS MORNING WILL STAY OFF THE STREETS. THIS WOULD BE A TREMENDOUS HELP.

With the actualities on cartridge tapes and ready for airing, Smith now begins to write stories about the snow storm, incorporating Carson's audio actualities. Smith's first story, which will air in his first newscast of the day, reports:

Smith: LAST NIGHT'S SNOW HAS CAUSED SLIPPERY STREETS THROUGHOUT MOST OF THE WEST SIDE. WAZY NEWS ASKED ROBERT CARSON, THE HEAD OF THE DEPARTMENT OF PUBLIC TRANSPORTATION, WHAT HIS PEOPLE ARE DOING TO EASE THE PROBLEM:
Audio Actualty: WE HAVE A NUMBER OF LARGE TRUCKS OUT, AND WE'RE SALTING THE AREA BEYOND THE INTERSTATE, AND WE'VE GOT TWO PLOWS SALTING THE MAIN STREET HILL AREA.
Smith: ROBERT CARSON ALSO SAID THE STOCKPILE OF SALT IS RUNNING LOW, AND MANY OF THE SALT TRUCKS ARE ALREADY IN THE GARAGE FOR SPRING MAINTENANCE. MOTORISTS ARE URGED TO REMAIN HOME UNLESS THEY MUST DRIVE.

The second story Smith prepares includes two audio actualities of Robert Carson and is somewhat longer than the first story. It begins with Smith reporting:

Smith: LOW SALT SUPPLIES AND SALT TRUCKS ALREADY IN THE GARAGE FOR SPRING MAINTENANCE. JUST TWO THINGS WHICH ADD TO THE PROBLEM OF KEEPING STREETS CLEAR ON THE WEST SIDE AFTER LAST NIGHT'S SPRING SNOW BLANKETED THE AREA. ROBERT CARSON OF THE DEPART-MENT OF PUBLIC TRANSPORTATION TELLS US:
Audio Actuality: WE TOOK TWO OF THE PLOWS OUT TO THE WEST SIDE, AND WE HAVE MEN OPERATING THEM TO TRY TO CLEAR A PATH FOR THE SALT TRUCKS, WHICH HAVE, BY THE WAY, THE LAST TWO LOADS OF SALT IN OUR STOCK-PILE, SO IT COULD BE A PROBLEM LATER THIS MORNING IF IT KEEPS SNOWING.
Smith: ROBERT CARSON, THE HEAD OF THE DEPARTMENT OF PUBLIC TRANSPORTATIOON, ALSO HAD SOME ADVICE ON HOW TO HELP WITH THE TRAFFIC PROBLEM.

Audio Actuality: HOPEFULLY, MOTORISTS WHO DON'T ABSO-
LUTELY HAVE TO DRIVE THIS MORNING WILL STAY OFF THE
STREETS. THIS WOULD BE A TREMENDOUS HELP.

The third story Smith uses is much like the previous two, except that
this one uses the actuality that hasn't yet been aired. What Smith is doing
is writing his story around the audio actualities he has collected. The story,
complete with audio actualities, is called a *wraparound* and is one of the
most common types of radio news production. Smith can incorporate the
actualities many different ways in the story by changing sentence structure
and rotating the actualities. All are acceptable as long as the story remains
accurate.

When working with actualities, edit the questions you asked out of your
audio and instead write them into your *dry copy* (radio news script). Follow those dry copy questions immediately with your interviewee's short
audio answers. For example:

Announcer: (Dry Copy) WE ASKED JONES HIS REACTION TO THE
RATE HIKE.
Audio Actuality: I THINK IT'S DEVASTATING. IT WILL RUN US
SMALL BUSINESS PEOPLE OUT OF BUSINESS.
Announcer: (Dry Copy) BUT DID JONES FEEL THE HIKE WILL
STIMULATE PRODUCTION?
Audio Actuality: ABSOLUTELY NOT.

This practice gives your newscast a professional sound and a quick tempo.

Preparing the Story

It would be impractical when writing your dry copy to include the entire
transcript of every audio actuality; that would be a waste of time. Since
you may not be the only person airing the story, however, you need to
include some basic information on your copy to other reporters who may
not be familiar with the actuality. For example, you or another announcer
will need to know exactly when an actuality ends and what the final words
or sounds on the actuality are in order to begin speaking immediately when
it concludes. It would sound rather strange for Bill Smith to air the actuality of Robert Carson and then wait for a few seconds to see if there are
any other comments recorded on the actuality. A simple cueing system is
needed to provide this information. It varies from station to station. Some
stations develop their own styles or abbreviations, which become standard
usage. A typical story with this information included is shown in Figure 6C.

Notice at the top of the story the words SNOW/MONDAY 5-6-77/WS.
This information tells what the story is about, what date it was written, and
the initials of the person who wrote it. Some stories also include informa-

```
SNOW  /  MONDAY 5-6-77/WS          KILL: Noon/Monday

    A LATE SPRING SNOW HAS BLANKETED THE WEST SIDE

    THIS MORNING.  MOTORISTS ARE LINED UP AT GAS STA-

    TIONS WAITING TO GET CHAINS ON THEIR CARS.  WGRE NEWS

    ASKED ROBERT CARSON, HEAD OF THE DEPARTMENT OF PUBLIC

    TRANSPORTATION, WHAT HIS DEPARTMENT IS DOING TO EASE

    THE PROBLEM.


          Robert Carson/7 sec./ We have a number....

                 ....the Main Street hill.


    ROBERT CARSON ALSO SAID THE STOCKPILE OF SALT IS RUN-

    NING LOW AND MANY OF THE TRUCKS USED BY HIS DEPART-

    MENT ARE ALREADY IN THE GARAGE FOR SPRING MAINTENANCE.

    HE'S URGING YOU TO REMAIN HOME THIS MORNING UNLESS

    DRIVING IS ABSOLUTELY NECESSARY.



                    # # #
```

tion on when a story should be killed (taken off the air), such as the notation, KILL: NOON/MONDAY. Sometimes stories need updating; for example, using the words THIS MORNING on a Tuesday newscast would not be correct. The information in the middle of the story tells which actuality will be aired (Robert Carson), how long it is (7 sec.), the first words of the actuality for the benefit of the person who will cue the actuality in the cartridge machine (We have a number . . .), and the final words of the actuality to prepare the announcer to begin speaking (. . . the Main Street hill.).

Quotes and Identification

In one of the above stories, Smith quoted Carson instead of using an audio actuality and read: ROBERT CARSON ALSO SAID THE STOCK-PILE OF SALT IS . . . Radio copy cannot use quotation marks in the same way that print journalism can. It would be very annoying if every time you quoted someone you said, ROBERT CARSON, QUOTATION MARKS, THE STOCKPILE OF SALT . . . or ROBERT CARSON SAID, QUOTE, THE STOCKPILE OF SALT . . . Instead, radio journalists simply say ROBERT CARSON SAID . . . Other leads to quoted material are: ROBERT CARSON ALSO TOLD WAZY THE STOCK-PILE OF SALT . . . or ROBERT CARSON ALSO EXPLAINED THE STOCKPILE OF SALT . . . or ROBERT CARSON TOLD US THE STOCKPILE OF SALT . . . The important thing to remember is to vary your introductions to quoted material. Just as it sounds strange to use the words, QUOTATION MARKS, or QUOTE, it is equally awkward to always introduce a quote with, JOHN DOE SAID.

Notice also that Smith mentioned Robert Carson's name *before* quoting him. Broadcast style does not identify the person after the quote. That style is left to print journalism, where it is possible to refer back to the quote after reading it. Thus, you would *not* write: THE STOCKPILE OF SALT IS RUNNING LOW, AND MANY OF THE SALT TRUCKS ARE ALREADY IN THE GARAGE FOR SPRING MAINTENANCE, SAID ROBERT CARSON.

Introducing Names and Titles

In the story about the snowfall, Smith introduced Robert Carson as ROBERT CARSON, HEAD OF THE DEPARTMENT OF PUBLIC TRANSPORTATION. Since Carson's title was long, it came after his name. If it had been short, then it could have preceded his name, such as SERGEANT ROBERT CARSON or RADIO DISPATCHER ROBERT CARSON. This rule applies to all radio news writing, not just when actualities are part of a story.

What about the titles Miss, Ms., or Mrs.? As a rule of thumb, if you don't know the person you're referring to in the story and therefore don't know by what title she prefers to be called, omit these social titles altogether. Write a woman's name into a story just as you would a man's, with both her first and last name. When you refer to her again in your story, refer to her by her last name. You're still being courteous to her.

Sources of Actualities

One of the most frustrating feelings a budding radio journalist may encounter is the thought that a day's news events do not lend themselves to actualities. Nothing could be further from the truth. Let's examine possible sources for actualities in the following examples:

An important person from your community has been injured in an automobile accident in a distant state. The information available to you includes the location of the accident and the name of the injured person. You may ask, "How can the dry details of this accident lend themselves to actualities?" As you seek to gain additional information about the accident, sources for actualities begin to appear. Some of them include:

1. The police officer investigating the accident.
2. The desk sergeant at police headquarters.
3. The radio operator at police headquarters having access to the information.
4. A passerby who may have witnessed the accident.

Consider another story: A bill pending in the state legislature concerns railroad pension benefits. Possible sources for actualities here include:

1. Representatives favoring and opposing the bill.
2. A lobbyist supporting the bill.
3. The author of the bill.
4. Local railroad workers.
5. The families of local railroad workers.
6. Retired local railroad workers.
7. Members of local railway unions.
8. Members of related professions explaining their pension plans, and follow-up reports comparing theirs with the railroad's.

Another example concerns an industrial accident in which two employees are injured by an explosion. Sources of audio actualities would include:

1. Eyewitnesses.
2. The plant public relations director.
3. Foreman or supervisory personnel.

4. Plant safety experts.

5. Plant officials.

6. Plant security personnel.

7. Safety experts not associated with the plant.

8. State safety officials.

9. Local safety officials.

10. Doctors, hospital workers, nurses, ambulance drivers, police, or fire-men who may have been involved with the accident in their capacity as rescue or treatment personnel.

Gathering Actualities

Any time you have the opportunity to gather information, you have the opportunity to gather actualities. The examples above are only a few of the unlimited possibilities. In seeking audio, you need to be aware that local actualities are relatively easy to obtain. The politician's statement, the mayor's reaction, and the police officer's description are all a telephone call away. Remember that telephone! It's an important aid. The telephone enables the radio journalist to contact news makers, record their comments, and air those comments without ever leaving the studio. Television can't begin to compete with this advantage. Learn to use and rely on the tele-phone. Along with saving time and energy, it will become an indispensable aid in doing your job swiftly and professionally.

PRODUCING A ROUND ROBIN

Another production process used in radio news is the *round robin*. It connects a series of live or prerecorded correspondent reports in a geo-graphical "circle" to provide full coverage of a given news event. The round robin begins and ends with the local station.

To better understand the round robin, we can liken it to radio coverage of a famous five hundred-mile auto race, in which an anchorperson is lo-cated in a central anchorbooth with four or five other reporters located around the track. The anchorperson reports the start of the race and then introduces the reporter on the first turn. After describing the race as it passes his vantage point, this reporter introduces the reporter on the second turn. This continues until the entire track has been covered, and the final reporter returns the broadcast back to the anchorperson. Al-though without the excitement of an auto race, a round robin works the same way, but instead of covering a race track, it covers a geographical area, such as a state, a county, or a city.

For example, consider a large city that has just been struck by a tornado. The radio station dispatches reporters to key areas in the stricken city. After briefly highlighting the tornado story in the news broadcast, the studio reporter introduces a newsperson located in the western part of the city, who reports via telephone on damage there. This newsperson then introduces a reporter in the north end of the city, who reports on that area. The process continues until all the reporters have aired their stories. In a live round robin, each reporter is equipped with a transistor radio and can take his or her cue to begin broadcasting directly on the air. The round robin works most effectively when a station has a large staff and good equipment or has a well-developed system of correspondents and stringers.

At a small station, the radio journalist may have to rely on prerecorded correspondent reports to produce the round robin. The process is not difficult, but does involve ingenuity and planning. The number of correspondents participating in a round robin is determined by the length or format of the newscast and the news value of a story. As an example, let's assume you want to provide a morning-after election summary of your entire state. You know many stories lie behind vote totals, and political analysts or reporters from each area have access to them. You decide to provide a complete analysis through a round robin. Before the newscast, you telephone a reporter at a cooperating radio station in a nearby city and arrange to record a report. We'll assume it's a city in the western part of the state called Elmville. After summarizing results of the election in her town, the Elmville reporter tags the report with: THIS IS JANE DOE, WAZY NEWS IN ELMVILLE. With this report recorded, you next contact a reporter in a northern city called Carsontown and record a similar report. The reporter in the northern city tags the story: THIS IS JOHN SMITH IN CARSONTOWN. WITH A REPORT ON THE ELECTION IN ELMVILLE, HERE'S JANE DOE. Notice that Smith tagged the report by introducing the Elmville reporter. Next you might add a report from the southern part of your state. You contact a reporter at a downstate radio station, who provides a summary from that city, which we'll call Center City. She tags her correspondent report: THIS IS SALLY RADIO IN CENTER CITY. AND NOW TO JOHN SMITH IN CARSONTOWN. You now have three prerecorded correspondent reports ready for your morning newscast. You begin your newscast with a story about the election in your own community. Then you say: WITH STATEWIDE ELECTION REPORTS, HERE FIRST IS SALLY RADIO IN CENTER CITY. You then air the prerecorded report from Sally Radio, followed immediately by the prerecorded report from John Smith, followed immediately by the prerecorded report from Jane Doe. Each correspondent introduces the next correspondent. After the final report, you continue the newscast.

You can develop a round robin around any story. Statewide reactions to important national or international events or even special features on summer vacations lend themselves to round robin productions.

PRODUCING MINI-DOCUMENTARIES

Radio news has sometimes faced a tough battle with other types of radio programming, especially music, because too many program directors have felt that news is more of a hindrance than a help in winning the ratings wars. In many cases their aversion to radio news has been justified. Most of them have been confronted by news directors bearing boring, thirty-minute documentaries, asking that they be aired and re-aired during prime drive-time programming. On anything but an all-news station or a station heavily oriented to news and information programming, such requests are less than welcome. In radio, most half-hour documentaries aired in their entirety lose a good many listeners unless the documentary is exceptionally exciting. Even a newspaper feature that takes a half hour to read tries the reader's patience. Most people either avoid such a feature or at least set it aside to finish later. On radio, that translates into shutting off the set or switching stations.

To avoid giving the listener these last two alternatives yet still provide news and information programming, the mini-documentary, or *mini-doc,* has become a favorite type of news presentation for many radio journalists. A mini-doc is not necessarily a short documentary, although it can be. Rather, it is a documentary presented in short (mini) parts, usually from two to five minutes in length. Each part is a self-contained presentation, yet it adheres to the theme of all the other parts. For example, a mini-doc on land-use planning might consist of ten parts, each three minutes long. Each part would deal with a particular land use problem.

To demonstrate how this process develops, we'll examine various plans of organization for mini-docs. You may have already encountered similar plans in English or speech classes. To be understood by its intended audience, a documentary must communicate a coherent and well-organized message, just as a speech or a well-written article does.

Plans of Organization

Plans for organizing mini-docs include chronological, problem-solution, geographic, cause-effect, and topical. Although in some cases these plans can be used together, try to avoid it, since this reduces the listeners' ability to understand the documentary. Because most parts run about three minutes maximum, combining plans within plans can be confusing and can focus the listener's attention on the organization of the mini-doc instead of on its message.

Chronological Plan. As the name implies, the chronological plan is based upon time. Perhaps you prepare a twelve-part mini-doc dealing with your community's urban development over the past year. You devote each part of the mini-doc to a particular month in that year. The chronological sequence works best when the mini-doc deals with historical material. Yet since many mini-docs deal with current topics, the time sequence is not a frequently used organizational plan.

Problem-Solution Plan. As the title here implies, the problem-solution plan analyzes a problem and provides a solution. No set rules decree how many parts of such a documentary should be devoted to the problem and how many to the solution; rather, the mini-doc's subject usually determines that. Various combinations and arrangements are possible, as long as the mini-doc is easy to follow.

Perhaps you want to produce an investigative documentary that deals with urban renewal in your community. Through your research you determine that three problems are involved: lack of government planning, lack of financing, and lack of sewage facilities. People in your community who are concerned with these issues feel they have solutions to these problems. For purposes of example, we'll assume their solutions propose formation of a new government body to handle urban renewal, cooperative financing by banks and government agencies, and issuance of bonds for a new sewer system. You decide your mini-doc will be presented in six parts—three devoted to an analysis of the problems and three devoted to an analysis of the solutions, presenting the pros and cons of each. We'll examine how these parts can be scheduled in Chapter 7.

Cause-Effect. Closely related to the problem-solution plan is the cause-effect plan. This is best understood by considering the effect first and then the cause, since the effect is usually more readily identifiable. A polluted river (effect) was *caused* by industrial waste. A higher urban crime rate (effect) was *caused* by a decrease in police patrols. Infant deaths in the local hospital (effect) were *caused* by suffocation. Arrangement of the parts of a mini-doc based on the cause-effect plan would be similar to the problem-solution plan. Three parts of the mini-documentary could investigate the cause, and three parts could investigate the effect.

Geographic Plan. When the subject of a mini-doc flows from one geographic area to another, you can use the geographic plan of organization. Suppose you decide to do a mini-doc on the plight of farmers who are facing a season of drought. The first part of the mini-doc deals with farmers in the northern part of your state, the second with the central area, and the third with the southern area. In this case, the organization flow was from north to south. Another organizational plan could develop from west to east. A good rule of thumb is to try to keep the organization in a straight line, permitting listeners to gain a visual image in their own minds. Avoid "hopscotching" from one area to another and then back again. Since you have a limited amount of time in which to present an important message, keep your organization simple.

Topical Plan. The topical plan is the most frequently used plan of organization. In this plan, each part of the mini-doc relates to a central theme, but they are not tied together by one of the plans previously mentioned. Or to put it another way, if the content of the mini-doc doesn't lend itself to any of the plans previously mentioned, then the topical plan is an other alternative. A topical plan permits the greatest flexibility. A mini-doc investigating a private school that is being run by parents might treat enough issues for a fifteen-part mini-doc. To develop that many parts along anything but the topical plan would be difficult. Similarly, the issue may not lend itself to any plan but the topical. Trying to force a problem-solution or cause-effect plan on a subject that really isn't a problem-solution or cause-effect concept would be senseless.

Writing the Mini-Doc

Rules for writing a mini-doc are the same as those for other radio news writing. The need to make your subject understandable and interesting is particularly vital, since you must retain the listener's attention over a longer period of time on a single subject than you would for a newscast.

An important consideration in writing mini-docs is the *transition* from one part to another—those all-important sentences that introduce and conclude each part of the mini-doc. In order for mini-docs to succeed, the listeners need an audible cue to carry them from one part to another, referring to what came before or what lies ahead. Consider the following first part of a ten-part mini-doc investigating a private school operated by a group of parents.

Announcer: SUNSHINE SCHOOL, A DOCUMENTARY INVESTIGATING AN ALTERNATIVE TO PUBLIC EDUCATION. OVER THE NEXT TWO WEEKS, WAZY NEWS WILL EXAMINE SUNSHINE SCHOOL. LOCATED ON THE OUTSKIRTS OF LINDEN COUNTY, SUNSHINE SCHOOL BEGAN IN 1976 WHEN A GROUP OF PARENTS BECAME DISENCHANTED WITH THE PUBLIC SCHOOLS AND DECIDED TO ACCEPT, ON THEIR OWN, THE RESPONSIBILITY FOR TEACHING THEIR CHILDREN. TODAY'S PROGRAM IS PART ONE OF A TEN-PART SERIES. OUR SUBJECT, HOW SUNSHINE SCHOOL BEGAN. . . .

Notice how the introduction presented us with four important pieces of information: First, it gave the title of the mini-doc and a brief explanation. Second, it told how long the documentary would be—ten parts— indicating that the subject would be treated in some depth. Third, it revealed how long the broadcasts would last—two weeks. Thus, if we were intensely interested in the subject, we would know how long to be on the alert to listen for all the parts. Fourth, it informed us that this was the first part of the series. If we had just tuned in to a mini-doc and heard the words PART THREE, we could, if we wished, contact the station for a transcript of those parts we missed. The information we still need to know is when the next part will be presented. That information will be aired in the conclusion:

Announcer: TOMORROW, WE'LL PRESENT THE SECOND OF OUR TEN-PART SERIES ON SUNSHINE SCHOOL. OUR SUBJECT TOMORROW WILL BE THE SUNSHINE SCHOOL CURRICUUM.

The conclusion told us that the next part would be aired tomorrow. In fact, it even repeated that important point. If it's Friday, and the program will not be broadcast on a weekend, the concluding sentence could merely substitute MONDAY for TOMORROW. If the second part of the documentary is to be aired later that same day, then this information would be included. TOMORROW would be replaced with IN THE NEXT HOUR or perhaps AT NINE THIS MORNING WE'LL PRESENT . . . We'll learn more about scheduling mini-docs in Chapter 7.

You can also vary your introductions and conclusions. You may wish to use production aids or musical news tones to precede and conclude each segment of the mini-doc. Their use in newscasts is discussed in Chapter 7. Or each part could begin and end with the name of the announcer, such as:

Announcer: THIS IS JOHN DOE. TODAY WE BEGIN A TEN-PART DOCUMENTARY ON SUNSHINE SCHOOL.

Another technique is to use an audio actuality as an introduction. In the case of Sunshine School, the voice of a teacher, a student, or a school official could launch each part of the mini-doc. After the actuality, the announcer introduces the program. However, the actuality should either be part of the documentary that is about to be aired, or relate directly to its subject matter. It's important to remember that these actualities and their transitions must be short, just as they are in a contemporary newscast. Even though you are presenting a subject in far greater detail than you would in a newscast, you still don't want to bore your listeners by airing the same voice for two or three minutes.

Particular sounds may also be used effectively in mini-docs. The roar of a tornado as an intro for a mini-doc about disaster relief for tornado victims or the wail of an ambulance siren as an intro for a mini-doc about paramedics are just two examples.

Using imagination and skill, you can think of many other types of writing and production techniques to employ. Mini-docs are becoming widely accepted, especially by stations that want to inform their listeners yet want to integrate that information into the delicate programming balance of music and commercial messages.

MOBILE NEWS

Advancements in electronic broadcasting equipment have made the use of the mobile news report an integral form of radio journalism. As defined in Chapter 5, a mobile news report is a live broadcast from the scene of news in the making, usually from a specially equipped vehicle. A live on-the-scene report of a coal mine disaster, a live report from a helicopter surveying traffic conditions, and a live report on skiing conditions from a snowmobile are all examples of mobile reports that become a regular part of radio newscasts. Mobile reports are not new to radio journalism. The networks were doing mobile reports in the 1930s from cars, ships, and planes.

The typical mobile news report consists of a reporter's succinct description of an event. The report will usually last from fifteen to forty-five seconds, much like an actuality. The length is important because most mobile news reports are broadcast as interruptions to the standard musical or commercial format of the station. Although you may feel certain events warrant expanded coverage, you must consider the overall format of the station. Except with such major events as disasters, two- or three-minute mobile news reports are simply not practical. A fuller description of the event can come in the regular newscast. Mobile news reports are usually preceded by a bulletin tone. The listening public gains respect for the tone and consequently increases its attentiveness when it sounds. Thus, the reporter doesn't need to recap information constantly in a mobile news broadcast.

A mobile news report is the same as any other story. All essential facts must be reported in a short period of time. The purpose of the mobile news report is to provide a capsule of information, not to substitute for a major newscast. On the other hand, you must be wary not to be brief to the point of creating alarm. Reporting a burning home and mentioning the city block where it's located but not the exact address can cause panic in every listener who lives on the block—especially if they're away from home and hear the broadcast. Of course, in some situations complete information is not available, yet the magnitude of the event necessitates airing a mobile report with only the information you do have.

The instant nature of radio prompts many instant decisions. You must choose between being first with partial information or last with total information. Your reporting credibility continually hinges in the balance between these choices.

The station's emphasis on news, the amount of news lending itself to mobile news reports, the content of news, and even the station format all determine how often mobile reports are aired. Experience suggests that the law of averages works with news as it does with anything else. A good news department, with consistent effort, can produce an approximately equal number of mobile news reports for any month. This does not mean that the reporter should scrape the bottom of the news barrel at the end of the month simply to meet some quota. On the other hand, significant news stories often do not become mobile news reports because reporters do not wish to expend the energy to go to the scene and cover them. Sometimes it is necessary to "dig" for mobile news reports in outlying rural areas. This actually improves the image of the station among its listeners. Although emergency services usually are the main source of mobile news, this does not have to be the case. A jury's decision on an important trial, a surprise announcement at a news conference, and other exciting events are all potential mobile news reports.

The audio wraparound discussed earlier in this chapter can also be incorporated into a mobile news report. To develop a wraparound, you need a cassette tape recorder. After you have recorded an interview, select a key actuality from that interview and cue the tape recorder to the beginning of it. Then begin your live mobile news report, describing the event and providing an introduction to the actuality. As soon as you introduce the actuality, push the "play" button on the cassette recorder, air the actuality, push the "stop" button, and continue with your mobile news report. If the cassette recorder is not directly connected to the transmitting system of the mobile news unit, you can place the mobile microphone or mobile telephone mouthpiece over the recorder's speaker and air the actuality in that manner. A tip—keep the volume low. The microphone will be directly over the speaker and the volume must be low to avoid overmodulation. If you hold the microphone away from the recorder, outside noise can interfere with the quality of the actuality.

In most cases, only one actuality will be used per mobile news report. To stop a cassette tape recorder at the end of one actuality and cut it to a second actuality, while simultaneously reporting a live description of a news event, takes dexterity and concentration that even the best radio journalists find impossible to master. The result is usually a sloppy report and considerable dead air. Some mobile news units have sophisticated audio-editing consoles that permit mobile reports to include more than one actuality, but these are the exception rather than the rule.

Beside being used as a bulletin interruption, mobile news reports can also be integrated into regular newscasts. For example, if the mobile report has been recorded, it's possible to use either the entire report or portions of it as actualities in subsequent newscasts from the studio.

Mobile reports have definite advantages. They show the listeners that the station is going the extra mile to provide the most comprehensive news coverage possible. Listeners soon realize that when they tune to a station, they will learn of news sooner than they could on stations that do not use mobile reports. When used responsibly, mobile news reports increase the professional stature and reputation of any radio news team.

STEREO NEWS

Stereo news provides listeners with an added dimension of sound that monophonic presentation does not. Stereo news does not offer additional information for the listener, but it does increase the vividness of radio journalism. It necessitates new skill on the part of the reporter, which, if used with professional expertise and artistry, can equal the creativity of television news photography.

To demonstrate the mechanics of stereophonic broadcasting and the way stereo news is produced, we'll examine the operation of the stereo FM receiver in your living room. Your stereo receiver is equipped with *two* distinct radio receivers, each one receiving a slightly different frequency. When stereophonc records are played, one track of the stereo record is broadcast on one frequency and the other track is broadcast on the other frequency. This same process is used for stereo news. Inside the studio, a stereo news presentation might consist of two news reporters alternating stories in a dual reporter format. The microphone of one reporter is connected to one frequency; the microphone of the other reporter is connected to the other frequency. At home, each frequency is received separately and fed into a separate speaker.

For the on-the-scene report, stereo news requires special equipment. Under monophonic conditions, a typical cassette recorder and a single microphone is all the equipment needed. However for stereo news, not only must the reporter be equipped with a portable stereo tape recorder, but he or she must also have a dual microphone system that can record stereo sound. One of the best dual microphone systems uses two highly directional microphones. For optimum efficiency, these two microphones need to be approximately six inches apart, point in the same direction, and have a one-inch thick styrofoam baffle between the microphones that extends approximately two inches beyond the mouthpiece. The styrofoam baffle helps to provide the sound separation necessary to achieve the stereo effect. One microphone should be flexibly attached so it can at times be pointed in an opposite direction. This flexibility allows the reporter to record an interview using one microphone for the reporter's voice and the other for the interviewee's voice. In some situations, a third microphone can be added. Consider the creative reporting capability this process provides at the scene of a parade: the reporter can use the single microphone to describe the parade, while two additional microphones pick up its full spectrum of sound. The growing popularity of FM radio and especially FM stereo will lead to a significant increase in stereo news reporting.

SUMMARY

Producing radio news calls for a special set of skills unique to the medium. First, it demands a condensed writing style and considerable rewriting. Second, it requires mastery of the use of actualities to transmit the actual voices and sounds of news in the making.

These basic skills can be combined into several techniques of radio production. Among them is the wraparound, which "wraps" a story around actualities, forming a composite news presentation. Another technique is the round robin, coordinating various correspondent reports in one newscast. The mini-doc breaks long radio news documentaries into short, complete capsules, each dealing with a separate segment of the mini-doc's overall theme. The mobile report combines capsuled news with actualities live from the scene of a news event. Utilizing the dual channel system of stereo adds new sound dimensions to radio journalism. All of these production techniques enhance the total presentation of a radio newscast.

SUGGESTED EXERCISES

1. Write four radio versions of the newspaper headline, "Light Turnout In Early Polls."
2. Record an interview with a local politician and select three actualities for use in a radio newscast.
3. These three actualities must now be condensed for use in a shorter newscast. Select the one you would use in the shorter newscast and explain the reasons for your choice.
4. Select a national wire service story and rewrite it to pertain to your local community.
5. Simulate a round robin by summarizing the week's events in your school or community. Designate an anchorperson and separate correspondents to write concise, forty-five second synopses of each day's events. Following the tagging procedure outlined in Chapter 6, coordinate the simulated round robin, beginning and ending it with remarks from the anchorperson.
6. Using the topic of "The College Press," develop themes for five mini-docs, each one of them organized according to a different plan (i.e.—chronological, problem-solution, cause-effect, geographic, and topical). List six specific parts into which you would divide each of these themes.
7. Take one of your organizational plans from Exercise 6 and write a complete mini-doc. Each of the six parts should be three minutes long and should incorporate four audio actualities.

chapter seven

Programming

A radio newscast is the sum of many parts. We've already discussed some of these—news sources, covering radio news, gathering radio news, and production. Another important aspect of a radio newscast is *programming*. Specifically, programming is the overall sound of the newscast and its smooth integration into the station's total audio image. The purpose of this chapter is to discuss those aspects of radio news that make it listenable.

ANNOUNCING THE NEWSCAST

There is no one style of announcing a newscast that is superior to all others. However, certain characteristics of the voice, qualities of expression, and word usage lend themselves to a more professional sound from the listener's point of view. A guaranteed step-by-step plan to perfect news announcing does not exist. Every radio reporter has his or her own individual personality, which is expressed in the voice. In some cases, that expression can be adjusted and improved, but to restructure it to the extent that a person's identity is lost is not desirable either. Improving your voice is possible if you first become aware of those qualities which *can* be improved and then gradually work on them. Training your voice for announcing is like physical exercise. You don't start by running the four-minute mile; that takes conditioning and practice. One way to start is to tape record your voice and then self-critique the playback. Another is to enlist an expert to critique your voice. But remember, good announcing is a continuing development process that demands practice throughout your career.

Although good announcing is helpful to the overall presentation of a radio newscast, the importance of voice quality can vary. At large metropolitan stations or all-news stations, as many as thirty different voices may be heard in a day, and every voice may not sound completely professional. A journalist's reputation for accurate and objective reporting can offset minor deficiencies in speaking. Moreover, a good voice only earns respect in radio news if the information communicated by that voice is objective and accurate. Usually, the emphasis on voice increases inversely to the size of the station's staff. If a news director of a small market station is the only news voice of that station, then it becomes relatively important that he or she be a good announcer.

Let's examine some of the qualities that help improve news announcing. Keep in mind that the material covered in this section is very basic. The serious broadcast professional will want to consult a text devoted entirely to announcing and may also want to study books that deal with the processes of voice and diction, as well as general speech communication.

Using Your Voice

As we noted earlier, the ideal method of analyzing and improving your voice relies on a critique by an expert and the use of a tape recorder. However, to better understand what that critique should involve, you should know something about the characteristics of the voice.

Every speaking voice has three essential characteristics: rate (how fast you speak), volume (how loud you speak), and pitch (the tonal intensity of your voice). We are all familiar with the phrase, "I could tell by the tone of his voice he was unhappy," or "He was almost shouting," or perhaps "He was talking so fast I couldn't understand him." These phrases reveal speaking characteristics in everyone's voice, and these attributes affect the quality of a radio newscast.

Rate. Of the three characteristics, perhaps the easiest one to control is rate, or how fast you talk. No mathematical formula specifies an ideal number of words per minute for a radio newscast.

Speaking too fast is one of the most common mistakes of beginning news announcers. A slower, conversational rate can be quite effective. Remember, people are listening primarily to what you are saying, and you have to speak slowly enough for them to grasp the meaning. After all, we don't talk to our friends at two hundred words per minute, and we shouldn't communicate to thousands of other people at that rate, either. Practice listening to yourself on the tape recorder and timing your normal speaking rate. Compare your voice with network announcers. Chances are that your voice can adapt to news announcing.

Volume. Volume is also easy to control, once you become conscious of it. Many beginning announcers feel that they can obtain a deeper resonance by artificially raising the volume of their voice while lowering the pitch. Such is not always the case. Many times the result is just that—a pronounced artificiality. Part of the problem stems from incorrect use of the microphone. The microphone can pick up a whisper, so you don't need to speak loudly when you are using one. The microphone captures and reflects every characteristic of your voice. It therefore magnifies any forced, unnatural sounds you might make by trying to speak louder than normal. When you're announcing a newscast, speak naturally. Speak loudly enough that a person twenty feet away can hear you. This will be sufficiently loud to project a quality of authority without seeming to communicate to an assembly hall.

Pitch. Unlike rate and volume, pitch is difficult to control. Here again a tape recorder and professional coaching are most helpful. Pitch variation occurs through either syllable emphasis or word and sentence emphasis. Monroe and Ehninger state:

> In connected speech, pitch is changed in two ways: (1) *by steps* and (2) *by slides*. For example, suppose someone has made a statement with which you agree, and you answer by saying, "You're exactly right!" The chances are that you will say something like this:

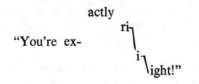

> The abrupt change in the word "exactly" is called a step, and the gradual change in the word "right" is called a slide.[1]

In announcing a newscast, you probably would not express nearly as much enthusiasm as the exclamation, "You're exactly right!" Nevertheless

[1] Alan H. Monroe and Douglas Ehninger, *Principles of Speech Communication* (Glenview, Illinois: Scott Foresman and Company, 1969), p. 110. The serious reader will want to consult Stuart W. Hyde's well accepted book, *Television and Radio Announcing* (New York: Houghton Mifflin, 1971).

the importance of pitch is in giving every word its individual tonal identity. We have all heard someone who speaks in a boring monotone. To avoid that, a constant self-monitoring process is necessary for a radio journalist who must announce a number of newscasts every day. Be careful not to let your voice fall subconsciously into a monotone and lose variety of pitch, or you will create the impression that you are not the least bit interested in the listener; you're just reading the newcast.

Pronunciation. Our discussion of pitch leads to another important consideration when announcing a newscast—correct pronunciation. Although it happens to every radio journalist, there is no excuse for mispronunciation. Correct pronunciation demands concentration and is especially important when you're new to an area. The pronunciation of many names and titles of local officials, buildings, and geographic areas is indigenous to a specific locale. The local pronunciation may be completely different from the standard pronunciation of the same word. Nothing labels a novice or outsider faster than mispronouncing the names of local officials or places. Similarly, nothing is more insulting to local ears than hearing the name of their home town or public official mispronounced. A golden rule of radio news broadcasting will normally prevent you from tripping on your tongue in these situations: *Read your copy before going on the air.*

Wire services have pronunciation guides they usually include with stories. For instance, if a revolution occurs in Africa, a special pronunciation guide for the country will be sent over the wire prior to stories about the revolution. In addition, most wire copy has a correct pronunciation guide after difficult words. A phonetic pronunciation commonly employed by Associated Press is shown in the following story from the broadcast wire:

(ADDIS ABABA) WITNESSES SAY ETHIOPIAN SOLDIERS EX-
CHANGED GUNFIRE WITH CIVILIANS EARLY TODAY IN STREET
FIGHTING ON THE SOUTHERN EDGE OF ADDIS ABABA (AD'-
IS A'-BAH-BUH), THE CAPITAL OF ETHIOPIA.

Many cities and geographic regions have names that are deceiving. Take, for example, the name, "Boise," the capital of Idaho. The pronunciation is "Boy'-see." However, in many areas of the country, the pronunciation "Boys" is common. Another example is the capital of South Dakota, the town of Pierre. The French pronunciation, and most common one outside of South Dakota, is "Pee'-air." However, the residents refer to it as "Peer." Localities bearing native Indian names are especially difficult to pronounce. An example is the town of Snoqualmie (Snow-qual'-um-me), Washington. Other difficult pronunciations include Hilo (He'-low), Hawaii and Okefenokee (Oak-kuh-fuh-noke'-key) Swamp, Georgia. The list is endless.

You must carefully check and re-check names and places for their correct pronunciation, for that, more than any other announcing flaw, points a direct finger at the amateur.

Enunciation. Enunciation refers to saying a word clearly and distinctly, giving emphasis to the identity of each syllable. Failure to enunciate properly can develop through weariness or lack of concentration. A tired newscaster will many times fail to enunciate clearly.

The danger associated with correct enunciation, however, is that we can sometimes overenunciate, resulting in a newscast delivery much like a phonetic exercise. Three sounds that are commonly overenunciated are the *T, S* and *P*. Budding news announcers tend to overstress these three letters. As a result, the sounds protrude beyond their natural range, so that the *T*s and *P*s produce popping sounds over the air, while the *S*s produce a distinct hissing sound. A microphone will amplify these abnormalities to sound like someone is spitting into it. One solution, although not totally adequate, is to move away from the microphone so that the air pressure between your lips and the diaphragm of the microphone is lessened. Some microphones have special filters to help eliminate these pops and hisses.

Accents. People in many sections of the country have distinctive accents that are indigenous to those areas. When newscasters from one area move to another location, their accents can be very noticeable. Often these accents can be overcome with practice. A strong regional accent is something the newscaster must guard against. Take, for example, the Brooklyn nasality or the Pittsburgh twang. If you live in these cities, listen carefully to local newscasters on small stations, and you'll often notice these distinct accents. The southern accent is even more pronounced. It's no accident that many successful news announcers come from the Midwest. That area of the country is considered to have one of the purest speech patterns in America. This in no way means that if you weren't born in Iowa, you'll never be a successful news announcer. It only means that if you do have a regional accent, you may have to work to overcome it by paying close attention to your speech patterns.

Pauses. Sitting in front of a microphone delivering a five- to fifteen-minute newscast several times a day can sometimes produce a tendency to daydream. As surprising as it sounds, every professional has had it happen. The result is a failure to pause sufficiently at punctuation marks, missing the emphasis on key phrases and sentences. Pausing at these punctuation marks demands concentration. It's easy to start listening to your voice instead of your news. In fact, you can become hypnotized by the sound of your voice. It becomes a continuous, soothing sound heard over an extended period of time in a sound-proof studio. This is one of the most subtle dangers associated with radio news announcing and can creep up on you without your knowledge. Some newscasters have actually read a story twice in the same newscast without realizing it, until the second reading was almost concluded.

Punctuation marks and emphasis on key words are important parts of the speaking process. Sentences are entities, and pauses mark entities within those sentences. Each of those entities must be given its own identity, or the meaning of the entire story is lost.

Style of Delivery

Along with the qualities of your voice, you must also be alert to pitfalls in your style of delivery.

The imitation. We all admire certain people. This admiration can creep into the subconscious of a news announcer. As an individual, it's important to remember that you are just that—an individual with qualities and characteristics all your own. Although you may subconsciously imitate the style of another newscaster, you should guard against it. This affects not only the beginning radio journalist; it can creep into a broadcast journalist's psyche after years of becoming complacent and relaxed in an announcing situation. Just as complacency and relaxation can cause missed pauses or punctuation marks, they can also cause a subconscious tendency to imitate, sometimes quite successfully, the voice of another newscaster.

American broadcasting personality David Brinkley has a very distinct announcing style. However, his ability to command the listener's attention has developed not only through his unique style, but also through his excellence as a journalist. Thus, the reporter who feels that the development of a unique style will guarantee success, without considerable journalistic training and professional experience, is living with an illusion.

Changing styles. The complacency that may result from repeatedly covering the same news beat and announcing the same daily newscast can also produce a change in announcing style. This is different from imitation. Style changes are more subtle, resulting in changes of rate, pitch, or tone of the speaking voice. It's a subconscious change than can develop from daily routine. Periodically recording and critiquing your voice is a good way to avoid it.

The ad-lib. Some veteran radio journalists find the ability to communicate information almost second nature. For them the typewriter becomes an instrument of shorthand rather than an instrument for composing a news story, and they rely on ad libs, or material composed as they speak. The reporter collects information for a story and types it before going on the air, but only uses it as notes to ad-lib a certain style and wording. Although the reporter may use the story three or four times a day, it is never exactly the same. In a sense, the reporter verbally rewrites the story each time he or she announces it.

Some reporters feel that the advantage of this type of announcing is that it allows them to concentrate on gathering news instead of rewriting it. Moreover, the ad-lib provides a conversational and, in some cases, more direct form of news presentation. Although some reporters find this ad-lib style easy and beneficial, others will have absolutely no part of it! The danger associated with it is clear—no direct control exists over what is being said. A change in a word, the slip of a tongue, an off-the-cuff innuendo, or an inflection in the voice can create an entirely different meaning and warp the story's accuracy. In extreme cases, careless ad-libbing may even result in a libel suit, to be discussed in Chapter 8.

A good rule of thumb for the ad-lib is not to use it except when absolutely necessary. Unless deadlines demand a story be aired before you have time to type it completely, a story should be typed in its entirety. The exception to this applies to mobile news reports, as discussed in Chapter 6. In this case, the reporter assigned to a mobile news unit usually does all of the reports ad-lib from notes or memory, a tough job under demanding situations.

The head bobber. Public speaking has taught us that we communicate with more than just our voices. Our facial expressions, our gestures, the nodding of our heads, and the expression of our eyes and faces all help to communicate information. For the radio journalist, however, the immediate feedback of interpersonal communication is absent. Even though you may be speaking to thousands or even millions of listeners, you cannot see these people. Your only feedback is the studio wall or perhaps the engineer in the adjoining studio. To compensate for this, you may visualize the presence of other faces and communicate with them with all the expression you would normally use in the actual physical presence of people. If it is not overdone, there is nothing wrong with this; in many cases it aids greatly in "feeling" the news that you're broadcasting and imparting realism to the typed copy. However, beware of bobbing your head in front of the microphone. Most broadcast microphones are designed to be effective when the mouth is approximately six inches away from the microphone's diaphragm. If your head bobs back and forth too much, the volume of your voice will fade in and out, and you will sound like you are announcing while spinning on a revolving chair. The key to overcoming this habit is simply to concentrate on keeping your head still. Many television newscasters with prior radio experience are seen on television with what is commonly referred to as a "radio head." Although the camera is taking a shoulder shot of the newscaster, his or her head is moving all over the television screen. Sometimes the desire to communicate the full meaning and expression of every word and phrase can send the newscaster's head literally out of control.

Air checks. We've all noticed how photographs may make people look different from what they imagine themselves to be. A woman's illusion about being slender can be quickly shattered by an objective snapshot. Think of the microphone and tape recorder in much the same manner as you would a camera. The tape recorder doesn't lie about your voice, and it's important that you continually take an audio picture, or *air check,* of your voice at least once every two weeks. Just as a video tape recorder can often pinpoint the flaws in a professional golfer's back swing, a microphone can pinpoint the flaws in a news announcer's voice. Listening to yourself doing a five- or ten-minute newscast can be a very revealing experience. Small speaking idiosyncracies can develop without your notice and can become accentuated and distracting to your audience. By air checking, you can keep your voice operating at its optimum level for effective speaking.

NEWS FORMATS

Radio is one of the most specialized of mass media. While some newspapers print special editions for different geographic areas, they don't have the means to specialize to their audience on a demographic basis the way radio does. Radio stations can tailor their formats to the black audience, Hispanic-American audience, teenage audience, religious audience, older American audience, upper income level audience, country audience, and many more. As these programming *formats* become specialized, especially in major markets, the news formats of the stations also become specialized.

We shall discuss radio news formats in terms of musical formats, but you should be aware that, although the news format tends to coincide with the musical format of the station, this is not the universal rule. News formats are also affected by such factors as market size, competition, personnel, and management.

Contemporary Formats

The contemporary format is geared to rock or top-forty music, and the news of contemporary stations is usually presented in a fast, compact style. The rate of presentation, in a sense, matches the tempo of the music. Most of the newscasts are no longer than five minutes and in many cases are much shorter. When headlines are aired at the half hour, they usually last from twenty seconds to one minute maximum. Some contemporary stations have special *news capsule* inserts that are even shorter than normal contemporary newscasts. They are aired in prime listening time and last from thirty to sixty seconds. Some contemporary stations even mention at the beginning of the news insert how long it will last, saying, "This news capsule has forty-five seconds of news, followed by more great music." The object is to retain the listener who listens to the station primarily for its musical programming, but who also wants to keep informed. Opinions vary as to the success, failure, or justification of the news capsule insert; nevertheless, these inserts are a way of life for some contemporary stations.

Public affairs programming on contemporary stations, although meeting FCC requirements, is often relegated to the hours between midnight and 6:00 A.M. or left to weekends. In major metropolitan areas, the content of the contemporary news format may stress police beat stories. The listenership of a contemporary station is a young audience whose members may not be attuned to community activities in the same way as the older adult audience. Chances are the listener has not been involved to a great degree in political activities, is not a tax-paying property owner, and therefore may not be vitally concerned with the political forces at work in the community. But even this is gradually changing. The lowering of the voting age to eighteen and the concern shown by young people over such issues as Vietnam, the environment, and social movements have directly affected the news programming of some of these stations. Stations and networks are responding to these changes by increasing their coverage of issues.

Networks frequently affiliated with contemporary stations include the Mutual Progressive Network and the American Contemporary Network, whose news schedules convey the shorter, more contemporary format. Mutual describes its news as:

A New Sound, that's Progressive/Comprehensive News. Economy of words. That's the fundamental approach and style. Network introductions and extra words have been eliminated; news begins each newscast.[2]

Affiliate stations can carry as little as a single minute of progressive news near the top of the hour.

The American Contemporary Radio Network bills itself as:

A nationwide lineup of stations with one thing in common . . . young adult and teen audiences . . . American Contemporary Radio Network offers news from a contemporary point of view.

[2] "Three Different Newscasts Each Hour," (prospectus), Mutual Broadcasting System, Inc., Washington, D.C.

News in a contemporary voice. . . . Features tailored specifically to the interest of younger audiences.[3]

Country/Western Formats

Country music is changing. Although the down-to-earth, foot-stomping twang of "blue grass" is still present, many country stations are country-rock and are similar to a contemporary station. Thus, news on country/western stations can either follow a contemporary format or be as "country" as the local folks like, dwelling heavily on hometown and farm-related news.

Middle-of-the-Road Formats

Middle-of-the-Road (MOR) radio stations air music that has a slower tempo and mood than music on contemporary formats. MOR stations are found in almost every market, regardless of size. The reason for this is that their "easy listening" music provides the widest demographic base of any radio format. You might ask, "Then why aren't all stations MOR?" Listeners still want a choice in radio programming, and when a market is saturated with one type of format, a fresh approach is welcome and profitable.

Newscasts on many MOR stations are more frequent and longer than those on contemporary stations. Because of the wide demographic base of the audience, the news coverage is often broader and more thorough. The content may include political, economic, educational, consumer, and special interest news. Longer newscasts permit more detail and an ample opportunity for more and longer actualities. Some MOR stations bring public affairs programming out of the night and weekend hours and air it with drive-time programming for listeners commuting to and from work.

Radio news networks frequently heard on MOR formats include the American Entertaiment Radio Network, NBC, CBS, MBS, United Press International Audio, and Associated Press Radio. These networks frequently present special features suitable for the MOR format, such as news commentary by noted network newscasters. Stressing the relaxed tempo of its extensive news coverage, ABC says of its American Entertainment Radio Network:

> Entertainment Radio correspondents, skilled at getting the news, provide comprehensive national and international news coverage in the manner of welcomed guests, not frantic speedsters.[4]

[3] "This Is The American Contemporary Radio Network," (prospectus), ABC Radio Sales Office, New York, September, 1972.
[4] "This Is The American Entertainment Radio Network," (prospectus), ABC Radio Sales Office, New York, September, 1972.

Classical Formats

Classical music stations provide soft background music to their listening audience featuring the works of classical composers. News on these stations can either be omitted or be limited to hourly newscasts usually lasting three to five minutes. Because of their emphasis on musical programming, classical stations may air very little local news and depend primarily on wire copy or networks news. An exception to this can occur when an FM station is part of an AM/FM complex and draws upon the news-gathering facilities of its AM counterpart. As a general rule, news programs on classical stations contain fewer audio actualities and use a much slower, mellower rate of delivery.

On some stations, public affairs programming is a regular feature. In fact, many classical music stations are public radio stations supported by public contributions and the Corporation for Public Broadcasting. They often subscribe to the National Public Radio (NPR) network. Programs such as NPR's *All Things Considered* are well-known and respected presentations on most public stations.

Information Formats

Except for all-news stations, radio's information format usually airs more news than any other. Many of these stations program an afternoon of MOR music with news and information blocks in the morning and evening drive-time. Some information formats include public opinion or phone-in programs during hours not covered by news or MOR music. Unless there's an all-news station, the information news team may be the largest in the local market. A typical news and information schedule during the drive-time hours usually consists of five to ten minutes of national news, an equal or greater amount of local and regional news, some sports, weather, and perhaps a special feature, such as business news or the stock market roundup. This schedule is usually repeated every half hour during drive-time.

Thus, a typical morning news block beginning at 6:00 A.M. could include the following program schedule:

6:00   National News
6:05   Local/Regional News
6:20   Sports
6:25   Business Report
6:27   Headlines in Review
6:28   Weather Roundup

6:30   National News
6:35   Local/Regional News
6:50   Sports
6:55   Business Report
6:57   Headlines in Review
6:58   Weather Roundup
7:00   National News

The schedule may continue to repeat itself until 9:00 or 10:00 A.M., when musical programming begins. Except for a noon newscast, music would continue until 4:00 P.M., when the news block would again be heard through 6:00 or 7:00 P.M.

An information format provides ample time for longer audio actualities. Some information stations have one or two reporters who concentrate solely upon gathering information and audio actualities. Their daily schedules follow those of any other member of the news team, except that they're primarily responsible for off-the-air reporting tasks.

An example of a network geared to this type of format is the American Information Radio Network, which has hourly newscasts lasting five minutes and in-depth reports lasting approximately twenty minutes.

All-News Radio

All-news radio stations have generally been located in markets with populations in excess of one million, primarily because the successful operation of an all-news station requires a sizeable population base to furnish enough listeners to make the station profitable. The total cost of operating an all-news station is approximately 60 percent higher than, for instance, an MOR station.[5] Needless to say, the total number of all-news radio stations is small. However, the advent of NBC's News and Information Service (NIS) is making all-news formats possible in much smaller markets. Carrying the NIS network for most of the hour reduces the station's expense of a massive staff.

Traditionally, the staffs of all-news stations are large and include many specialty reporters. Individual reporters are often assigned to cover specific areas exclusively, such as education, the courts, police, business news, or consumer affairs. Special features, in-depth documentaries, and longer interviews are prevalent in all-news formats.

The formats of all-news stations vary considerably, but generally follow a "dartboard principle"—dividing each hour into pie slices and scheduling

[5] "The All-News Way of Radio Journalism," *Broadcasting*, 88, no. 1 (January 6, 1975), p. 36.

specific news or features in each slice. National, international, local, and regional news slices, as well as sports and weather slices, are heard during each hour, much like drive-time information formats. During the early afternoon, some stations adjust the size of the slices for longer in-depth features. All news stations are the most likely ones to provide continuous coverage of such major events as Presidential news conferences.

Some all-news radio stations are owned by networks. CBS owns five, and Westinghouse, three. The popularity of all-news stations has increased significantly in recent years. News of international diplomacy, political developments in Washington, and the economy have all made us a news-conscious people who constantly monitor information that significantly affects our lives.

You can discover other specialized radio formats by turning any radio dial. Some stations even combine various formats within the same programming day: such as MOR in the morning, jazz or classical in the afternoon, and contemporary in the evening. No universal rules exist by which to fit radio news neatly to a particular format. However, either through local announcers or a network, most stations attempt to integrate the presentation of news into the total image of the station.

SCHEDULING

Scheduling is the position, time, and content of the locally produced newscast in relation to other radio programming. For example, some stations air their newscasts on the hour, others air them five minutes before the hour, and still others air their news at fifteen minutes after the hour.

Positioning Around Networks

Much like formats, scheduling too depends upon many factors in a station's overall operation, of which news networks are a major determinant. Some news or program directors like to coordinate the local newscast around the network news schedule. If, for example, the network airs news at five minutes before the hour, then the local news is presented immediately preceding or following network newscasts. One variation of this schedule is the presentation of local headlines just before the national network news, with the complete local newscast following the network news. If the local station carries network news on the hour as well as network headlines on the half hour, then scheduling local news next to network headlines is a common practice.

Another common news schedule is to place the local newscast directly "opposite" the network newscast; that is, if the network airs news at five minutes before the hour, the local report will air at twenty-five minutes after the hour, exactly opposite the network news on the clock. Some stations prefer this opposite schedule, since it permits news to be spread out over the hour rather than having it bunched into one time period.

At some stations, local newscasts promote stories to be featured in the upcoming network newscast. Similarly, short headlines can follow a network newscast to promote the next local newscast. These short promotional headlines, or *news teasers,* can be prerecorded. For example, an on-the-hour local newscast plus prerecorded headlines at fifteen, thirty, and forty-five minutes after the hour provide sufficient news promotion yet enable the news staff to spend its time following up on story developments, rewriting, and gathering audio actualities. Promotional announcements can sometimes be inserted in a national network newscast when the local station is not obliged to carry the commercial or public service announcement aired by the network. In this instance, at the cue for the network public service announcement, the local news announcer will break in with one minute of local headlines. That announcer may close by saying something like, "Stay tuned for complete details after NBC news."

Scheduling Mini-Docs

Mini-docs, as discussed in Chapter 6, can be scheduled two ways— vertically and horizontally. Vertical scheduling airs all parts of the mini-doc during the course of the same day. Horizontal scheduling airs one part of the mini-doc on one day (usually more than once), the second part on the next day, and continues this process until all the parts have been aired. A station usually schedules mini-docs with greater frequency during drive-time periods. An exception to this might be those mini-docs designed particularly for the homemaker, who may be the prime listener during mid-morning and early-afternoon periods.

A common scheduling procedure is to air mini-docs directly adjacent to or in the middle of regularly scheduled newscasts. In order to do this, time limitations demand that the newscast be at least five minutes long, and each part of the mini-doc be not over two minutes long. A station airing six major newscasts per day can use horizontal scheduling, repeating the first part of the mini-doc in or adjacent to every newscast. Or a vertical schedule can air different, consecutive parts of the mini-doc in or adjacent to every newscast. Whichever way your station schedules mini-docs, make sure that your listeners know when the next part will be aired. It's unnerving to listen to one part and never hear a mention of when the next part will be broadcast. It's much the same as airing one part of a prime-time movie on television and never mentioning when the next part will be aired.

You can also combine these scheduling procedures, especially when you use problem-solution or cause-effect organizational plans. Our earlier example of a six-part mini-doc on urban renewal applies here. Assume the first part of the mini-doc dealt with the problem of financing urban renewal, and the second part dealt with possible solutions to the financing problem. If this financial issue was complex and it was necessary for the listener to hear the first part (problem) in order to understand the second part (solution), then both the first and second part could be scheduled on the same day. Parts three (problem) and four (solution) dealing with another aspect of urban renewal could be scheduled on the following day. Parts five (problem) and six (solution) dealing with a third issue could then be scheduled on the third day. The two parts (problem and solution), although not scheduled back to back, could be separated by a half hour of prime morning programming. This whole process (problem, half hour, solution) could then be repeated later in the day. Similar arrangements would apply to cause-effect plans.

The key in scheduling mini-docs is to air the different parts of the mini-doc in an arrangement that makes the subject matter understandable to the listener. If the listener has an opportunity to hear all parts of the mini-doc and understands the issue being reported, then the scheduling is successful.

Major News Presentations

The number of major local news presentations per day, usually ten to fifteen minutes or more in length, will vary from station to station. The news and program directors must first determine if a major morning, noon, and evening newscast will adequately meet the needs of their coverage area. This decision is based on such considerations as market size, competition, format, personnel, and budget. At some stations, a shorter local newscast may be placed near one of the major newscasts, so that, if the major morning newscast airs from 8:00 A.M. to 8:15 A.M., a five minute local newscast may be heard at 7:30 A.M. and 8:45 A.M., and then none until the major noon newscast. A similar schedule may be bunched around the major noon and evening news presentations. Stations that command a large share of the late evening audience (those persons listening after 9:00 P.M.) may need a major summary newscast around 11:00 P.M. These are often recorded earlier in the evening. When they are presented live, these late newscasts present an excellent opportunity to report news and information six hours before the morning edition of the newspaper hits the streets. The midnight newscast also provides an opportunity for the earliest news about community evening meetings.

Effects of the Locale

Scheduling can also be affected by the particular characteristics of each locale.

Market size. Market size is one important consideration. Small and medium market stations will usually have two or three major local daily newscasts with perhaps two shorter local newscasts. At some stations, no other news will be heard except during the two daily drive-times. In a sense, these radio stations' news schedules resemble the news schedules of a television station. As market size increases, the increased competition will often force stations to schedule some form of local news at least every hour.

Competition. News competition from other radio stations influences scheduling in other ways. In large multi-station markets, you can spin the radio dial and find radio news almost any minute of the day. Although your market may consist of ten or more radio stations, you actually compete directly with only one or two stations. The competition might be the station with a news format like yours; it might be the station closest to you in the latest ratings; or it could be the station that programs the same music as your station.

In most instances, scheduling with an eye on the competition means locating newscasts in the general proximity of, but not directly overlapping, the competition's newscast. For example, if the competition schedules a major newscast at 8:00 A.M., your major newscast might begin at 7:55 A.M. If the competition schedules its major morning newscast at 7:30 A.M., yours might start at 7:00 A.M. or, if that's too early to reach most of your audience, 7:25 A.M.

If your station's local news team commands significant listenership, respect, and credibility, your local news can be programmed simultaneously against the network news of another station. Except when crises occur, hometown news will usually carry greater impact than national or international news. Thus, when a successful local news team is developed, this news schedule can be a powerful tool of competition.

Only when your local news gains the acceptability and listenership to almost dominate a market can you begin to schedule your local newscasts simultaneously against competing stations' local newscasts. When a significant margin of news superiority has developed in any market, the station on top can force the listeners into making a choice between stations. Once that choice emerges, it can be difficult to reverse.

Some radio stations schedule news to compete with the local television news. In these situations, the station usually schedules its radio news before the local television news, and makes every effort to report stories likely to be aired on the local television station. In markets where the closest competition is a television station, radio news aired before the television news gives the radio medium an advantage.

In some small markets, the newspaper can become the object of competition. When this happens, your radio station cannot report stories in greater detail than the newspaper but it can carry stories the newspaper may have missed, airing them before the newspaper is off the press. The immediate coverage quality of radio is a significant advantage in competing with a newspaper, since a story breaking just before press deadline forces the newspaper to give it only token coverage. Meanwhile, the radio news team has twenty-four hours in which to cover the story thoroughly before the newspaper can run another edition. When the newspaper tries to report the same story in more depth, this "second day" coverage is usually old news.

The length of a local newscast can also be determined on the basis of competition. If the competition customarily airs three- to five-minute newscasts, your station may schedule a more extensive newscast either adjacent to or simultaneous with the competing station, permitting more stories in greater detail.

Traffic flow. The size of a market and the general location of industrial and residential areas determines the traffic flow patterns within the market area. Traffic flow is important because it determines what hours of the day a substantial segment of the population is commuting to work—usually by car and usually listening to their car radios. The value of traffic flow data is to schedule newscasts in the morning and evening to match these prime drive-time hours. With this in mind, some metropolitan radio stations schedule hour-long newscasts during drive-times to reach commuting workers. Morning drive-time, although listed on many station rate cards or advertising brochures as lasting from 6:00 A.M. until 9:00 A.M., usually peaks between 7:00 A.M. and 8:30 A.M. It is during this time that most people leave home in order to reach work by 8:00 or 9:00 A.M. Morning drive-time newscasts give these people an opportunity to hear at least one major local newscast before entering the office or factory.

The work force. Like traffic flow patterns, the work force of a community will also affect news schedules. For example, a community may be highly industrialized, with manufacturing plants and assembly line factories operating one to three daily work shifts. In this setting, the drive-times of the community may peak at 7:00 A.M., 3:00 P.M., and 11:00 P.M., the hours of shift changes.

Similarly, in a predominantly agricultural market, the farmer is an early riser. During harvest or planting season breakfast is at 4:00 or 5:00 A.M., and by 6:00 A.M. many farmers are in the field. In such markets, stations often schedule a major morning newscast at 5:00 A.M. In markets bordering agricultural areas, morning news may begin at 4:00 or 5:00 A.M. and be repeated on the hour to reach both the agricultural and the business communities.

When scheduling news, it's important to take into consideration all of the above factors. Certainly every situation is different, and some factors will play more important roles than others. All, however, must be examined in order to reach the widest listening audience.

COORDINATING THE NEWSCAST

Coordinating a radio newscast means organizing the various sections of the news—local, regional, national, international, sports, weather, features—into a total, professional presentation. For instance, a typical fifteen- to thirty-minute newscast could begin with local news, turn to regional news, and close with national news, followed by a sportscast, special consumer affairs report, business news, or stock market report. Coordination also depends on whether or not the station subscribes to a news network. If it does, the local news team may not report much national and international news, leaving that instead to the network.

Some radio stations may subscribe to regional news networks. As described in Chapter 1, these networks are designed for a geographic region, such as the South, and permit the local news team to concentrate exclusively on local news, leaving both regional and national news to the networks.

Many of the factors that influence news scheduling also influence news coordinating. For instance, if a competing station begins its newscasts with local news, you must then decide whether to compete directly with it and begin your newscast with local news, or instead begin with national or international news.

Size of the market also influences coordination. Small markets permit a radio station to be a significant news force in the community and to dominate much of that market's news output. The type of news also varies. It is not unusual for small market radio stations to include obituaries in the local newscast, giving biographic details and funeral arrangements. School lunch menus and service club meeting notices are also familiar items on small market stations.

Some difficult programming decisions arise when small markets move into a period of rapid growth. A radio station catering to a small community may, over a period of a few years, find itself broadcasting to a medium-sized market with a different set of information needs. Competition may also have arrived. The established station must now decide whether to continue the successful "small town" news format or venture upon an image change. Whatever the decision, it is indeed soul searching and risky.

Unique community characteristics are also a factor in coordinating newscasts. In a predominantly agricultural region, the weather is a very important item and receives considerable coverage. If a radio station is located in a college or university town, then news concerning the university will be included.

EQUIPMENT LAYOUTS

Well-designed equipment layouts are essential to successful programming. This is true in all phases of radio station operation, and news is no exception. In the majority of stations, the on-air reporter is responsible for *switching* his or her own newscast. That means the reporter not only announces the news, but also operates the tape machines to air actualities and commercials. Having equipment easily accessible for fingertip operation when simultaneously announcing a newscast is therefore a critical part of the programming process.

In most newsrooms, the equipment layout will consist of a small, fairly compact control console. By compact, we mean smaller than the control console in the station's main control room. A newscast does not require as many "channels" of operation as a typical disc jockey program. Thus, the news control console will usually have a minimum of five audio controls, called *pots*. One will control the reporter's microphone. Another may be connected to the telephone line to record local actualities or actualities fed from the network. A third and fourth may be connected to cartridge tape machines. The fifth pot will usually be the master control.

The cartridge tape machines are usually located directly adjacent to the control console. Multi-cartridge machines permit the news announcer to load a number of the audio actualities before beginning the newscast. In other words, if a newscast has twelve audio actualities, one actuality is recorded on each cartridge tape. The twelve cartridge tapes are then loaded into perhaps four cartridge tape players, each capable of handling three cartridge tapes. Then the news announcer can air twelve audio actualities without ever having to change cartridges.

To keep the reporter from stretching away from the microphone in order to operate the cart machines, some stations have installed remote switching systems directly in front of the news control console. Five, ten, or even fifteen silent mercury switches can be installed, and the reporter can then switch the entire newscast with relative ease.

A telephone and typewriter are also necessary equipment and should be in easy proximity to the control console and recording devices. The newscaster should be able to record an actuality, turn to the typewriter, and type the copy for that actuality without leaving his or her chair. The telephone should be located close enough to the typewriter so that the reporter can type stories while still keeping the telephone to his or her ear.

Good lighting and acoustics are other primary requirements for any news room. A bold-faced or digital clock in a central location and filing cabinets or a storage area are also important. A board with heavy duty clips should be located near the wire service machines on which to organize the various national, regional, local and other categories of news copy that come over the wire.

Ideally, the station should provide separate offices or working areas for every member of the news department. Each office should have a desk, telephone, typewriter, and in larger stations, a recording and editing system. These offices, of course, should be located as close as possible to the main news studio.

Sound-proof cases permit the teletypes to operate in the news studio without making excessive noise, although some stations prefer the noise, utilizing it as a background sound effect. The new silent teleprinters eliminate the need for sound-proof housings.

SWITCHING THE NEWS

At stations where the reporters have sole responsibility for switching the newscast, they can usually provide tight transitions between voice and actualities in the newscast. The reporters know, having recorded their own actualities, that if a certain actuality has a split-second lead, the introduction must be timed accordingly. The key to switching is to eliminate any *dead air* (silence) in the newscast. For example, the sound of a politician's voice on an actuality should begin a fraction of a second after the newscaster concludes the introduction to that actuality. When the last sound of that politician's voice is heard, the newscaster's voice should immediately follow. Any pause longer than a split second is noticeable to the listener. Just as television audiences are annoyed at delayed news film, bad camera shots, or visuals that don't coincide with the stories, radio audiences are equally annoyed at sloppy news switching. In cases in which two people are involved in the switching process, sometimes an almost psychic rapport develops between the two. For instance, if an engineer switches the news, the reporter's specific writing style and production technique become so familiar that the engineer can almost anticipate every pause, hesitation, and cue. This empathy is especially important in using actualities.

When writing and coordinating your newscast, you must consider the electronic capabilities of the station. Suppose you have written a news story around two audio actualities that are scheduled back-to-back. If you are not using cart machines with multi-cart capabilities and don't allow enough time in your story to change tape cartridges, a considerable amount of dead air will result. In this instance, it would be wise to place the two audio cuts on a single cartridge. You may ask, "If recording two audio actualities on one cartridge tape is easier for switching purposes, why not put all of the audio actualities on a single cartridge?" The first reason for not doing so is that in a busy news room, recording is a very time-consuming process. Second, recording on one cartridge does not permit revising news stories or rearranging their order in the newscast without completely rerecording the master tape. Third, if a switching mistake is made or an actuality erroneously recorded out of order, it's impossible to compensate for these mistakes and rearrange stories and actualities in the middle of the newscast when all of the actualities are on a single tape.

Although switching the newscast may at first seem of little concern to the total news-gathering and writing process, it is the secret to airing a professional-sounding newscast. All the effort of gathering and writing news will lose its impact and turn into a comedy of errors if the newscast is not switched with precision.

COMMERCIALS

The placement of commercials within a newscast varies according to the newscast's length, the number of sponsors, and the length of the commercials. Most five-minute radio newscasts have only one sponsor, and the total commercial content within the newscast adds up to one or two minutes. An additional commercial may appear at the beginning and the end of the newscast, incorporated into the *intro* and *outro*. For example, a typical introduction for a radio newscast sponsored by a lumber company might read:

THIS NEWS IS BROUGHT TO YOU BY THE EIGHTY-FOUR LUMBER COMPANY, WITH THE MOST COMPLETE LINE OF LUMBER SERVICES AND SUPPLIES, LOCATED FOR YOUR BUSINESS CONVENIENCE ON THE SQUARE IN DOWNTOWN KANSAS CITY.

A similar announcement would be incorporated into the newscast's outro.

The actual placement of the commercial within the newscast is a decision made cooperatively between the program director and the news director. The station's account executive may also have a say in this decision if the commercial has been sold to air at a specific time, such as the center of the newscast or directly after headlines. Some newscasters welcome a break in the middle of their newscasts to give them a breather. A five-minute newscast will therefore usually place a commercial one to two minutes into the presentation. The timing is not exact but rather approximate, coming midway through the newscast at the end of a news story. This commercial placement can be a natural break between local, regional, or national news. If, for example, national news is aired first, followed by regional and local news, a commercial might be placed at the end of the national news and another at the end of the local news. Some newscasters prefer to air commercials first and then present a complete newscast unbroken by commercial sponsorship. In these cases, one commercial will usually follow the lead headlines; the second commercial may close the newscast directly before the weather.

Some station policies prohibit certain commercials, based on the content of the news. For example, one radio station's policy considers it in bad taste to run an airline commercial when a story about an airline crash is in the news. Other stations have policies of not airing automobile commercials when a traffic fatality is in the news. These are decisions that rest with the programming, news, and sales departments and, in some cases, the sponsor. Opinions vary on the ethical merits or acceptability of such policies, but they nevertheless do exist at some stations.

USING PRERECORDED MATERIAL

Politicians, government agencies, private businesses, and trade associations sometimes record various messages about current issues and make these available to anyone who wants to dial a specific telephone number. A recorded device is triggered to play these messages. In essence, they are public relations devices to present a particular point of view. Some radio news departments were in the habit of calling the numbers, usually toll free, recording the information, and then airing it in their newscasts. The FCC, however, stepped in and notified stations in 1973 that it expected an identification in the newscast whenever such prerecorded material was used. Thus, if you call Washington or anywhere else to obtain a prerecorded message about a political or controversial issue, you must announce that the statement was *furnished* to you by whoever was responsible for producing it. You can't claim that your news department interviewed the politician, which is not true. Although the telephone message is the most common form, this same policy applies to any prerecorded material, regardless of how it's received. Politicians frequently send stations prerecorded audio tapes with the politician's comments on current issues. The comments usually last between thirty and sixty seconds, ideal for use on a radio newscast. The FCC does not prohibit the use of such material but does require that you make the proper announcement before it is aired.

SIMULCASTING

Simulcasting is the process of airing a newscast on more than one radio station at the same time. An example is an AM station's newscast broadcast simultaneously on its FM counterpart. Simulcasting is the exception rather than the rule; most newscasts are heard only on one medium at one time. When simulcasting does occur, the news team must carefully consider special programming needs, especially station formats. An AM contemporary station may have a classical FM counterpart; in this instance, the newscaster must make the decision to either program to one station or the other, but not to both. Attempting to split the difference between the two stations in order to retain the image of each may have the effect of weakening the total presentation.

AUTOMATION

Technical developments in automated broadcasting equipment have made the automated radio station commonplace. For the radio journalist, however, automation has not significantly changed the news-gathering or reporting process. The automated station operates with a series of cartridge tapes and/or long reel-to-reel tapes cued to automatically air commercials, music, and prerecorded newscasts. If an automated station prefers live newscasts, the engineer can simply switch from the automation to the news studio at a specific time, and the local reporter can present a live radio newscast. When the newscast is over, the station returns to automation. If the news too is prerecorded, then an entire newscast, complete with commercials, audio actualities, intros, and outros, is recorded on a single cartridge tape or series of cartridge tapes. These tapes are then inserted into the day's sequence of programming tapes or reels, and cued to air at a specific time of the day. The advantage of automation lies in its ability to produce very high quality precision formats; it eliminates the human error factor in switching and the salaries of disc jockeys.

PRODUCTION AIDS

Transition between the musical programming and the news programming of a station should be as smooth as possible. To provide this, stations use professionally produced production aids, commonly called *jingles,* which are the "sounds between the sounds." They are usually separate musical tones inserted between the end of a song and the start of a newscast. These aids are also used to introduce special types of news programming, such as news bulletins, mobile news reports, election coverage, and sports coverage, all providing one identifiable introduction to news presentations.

SUMMARY

Radio news programming relies on certain elements to integrate the sound of news into a smooth transition with the rest of the station's programming and present a total, professional sound to its listeners. Among those elements is announcing, and its qualities of correct pronunciation and enunciation. Radio news formats play a vital role in programming, for news content and delivery are often paced to blend with the station's musical programming. Scheduling determines when newscasts will be aired in relation to the rest of the programming, concentrating on such factors as market size, competition, traffic flow, and community characteristics. Another element, coordination, is the organization of the various newscast segments, such as local, regional, national, international, sports, weather, and features.

The location of equipment in the newsroom and its proper use in switching the newscast can make the difference between a professional sound or a sloppy broadcast. Integrating commercials into the newscast is another important element of programming. When using prerecorded material, the FCC requires an announcement that the material was furnished to the station by the party involved. At some stations, news is simulcast, that is, aired over more than one station at the same time. Also, newscasts are part of the regular programming of automated stations. Production aids or jingles provide smooth, easily identified transitions between the music and the newscast or bulletin.

SUGGESTED EXERCISES

1. Record your voice as you read two wire service stories. Have a friend note on a checklist if you do any of the following: speak too fast; fail to pause at punctuation marks; mispronounce words; overenunciate *S*s, *T*s and *P*s; bob your head; or speak with a noticeable accent.

2. Interview the radio news directors of a contemporary and an MOR radio station. Ask them how they schedule their local news presentations to blend with the station's total programming.

3. Interview two radio news directors in your area and find out how their station's local news is scheduled in relation to their station's network programming.

4. Record five newscasts of various lengths aired on local radio stations. Time the length of each story. Do the stories differ in length? Why?

5. Monitor five stations that can be heard clearly on your radio. Keep a diary of what time of the hour and day they air their major newscasts. Compare how long the newscasts are, what national radio news networks are heard on the station, when local newscasts are aired, and how they schedule their commercials within their newscasts.

chapter eight

Regulation

The regulation of radio journalism stems from a unique set of characteristics inherent in the radio medium. First of all, radio is fairly young compared to books and newspapers. Many legal statutes concerning the press were decreed before radio was created. In addition, the courts are in the process of re-evaluating their attitudes about this complex new electronic journalism. Also, airwaves don't conveniently stop at geographic boundaries, thereby creating both interstate and international problems. For instance, powerful West Coast stations are required to cut back power at night to keep them from interfering with Canadian and Mexican stations. Most important, the number of radio frequencies is limited, necessitating control of their use. For the above reasons, the FCC, Congress, and professional journalism organizations have interpreted, enacted, and suggested a body of regulations for radio journalism.

THE FCC

The origin of the Federal Communications Commission can be traced back to America's first radio law, the Wireless Ship Act of 1910, which gave the Secretary of Commerce and Labor jurisdiction over emergency communication devices for ocean vessels. Realizing that this new medium would soon grow far beyond maritime use, Congress enacted the Radio Act of 1912, which required all radio stations to be licensed by the Secretary of Commerce. However, this Act did not give the Secretary of Commerce any authority to assign specific wave lengths, to determine times that a station could broadcast, nor to allocate a specific amount of power to each station for transmission.[1] The resulting chaos was a jumble on the radio receiver.

Congress next created the five-member Federal Radio Commission with the Radio Act of 1927. This Commission was a temporary agency with its authority tempered by public convenience, interest, and the necessity to regulate the broadcasting industry more fully. Its members were appointed by the President with the advice and consent of the Senate. One member was appointed Chairman by the President. The Act gave the Commission the right to review broadcasting licenses every three years. The Communications Act of 1934 changed the Commission's name to the Federal Communications Commission (FCC), increased its size to seven members, and established it as a permanent regulatory agency to "regulate interstate and foreign commerce in communication by wire and radio." [2]

The FCC is not an actual court of law, and its decisions must be made within the provisions of judicial statute and mindful of the Constitution. For example, if the FCC decides that a broadcast license should be revoked, it cannot do so without first holding a hearing on the matter, as required by the Administrative Procedures Act. After a series of hearings and rehearings have been held, the licensee in question can still appeal the FCC's decision to the United States Court of Appeals for the District of Columbia, and eventually to the Supreme Court.

In its relations with radio news, the FCC is explicitly prohibited from censoring free speech by the Communications Act, which in Section 326 states:

> Nothing in this Act shall be understood or construed to give the Commission the power of censorship over radio communications or signals transmitted by any radio station, and no regulation or condition shall be promulgated or fixed by the Commission which shall interfere with the right of free speech by means of radio communication.[3]

However, the Commission does define news in its program log regulations by stating that news programs:

> . . . include reports dealing with current local, national, and international events, including weather and stock market reports; and

---

[1] William J. Donovan, Acting Attorney General, *Attorney General's Opinion*, 35 Ops. Att'y Gen. 126, July 8, 1926, Reprinted in: Frank J. Kahn, ed., *Documents of American Broadcasting* (New York: Appleton-Century-Crofts, 1968), p. 31.

[2] *The Communications Act of 1934*, Title I, Sec. 1, Public Law 416, 73d Congress, June 19, 1934 (Amended to December, 1964).

[3] *The Communications Act of 1934*, Title III, Part I, Sec. 326.

when an integral part of a news program, commentary, analysis, and sports news.[4]

The Commission further spells out "the major elements usually necessary to meet the public interest, needs and desires of the community in which the station is located" for the fulfillment of the licensee's obligation to the community, and news is among the elements.[5]
In addition, it states that:

> Certainly, the establishment of sound station policy with respect to news, information, and the discussion of public issues is a major factor in operation in the public interest.[6]

The agency then reviews whether or not the licensee has lived up to its obligation through these programming elements, and from that review, determines license renewal. The Commission does stress, though, that those elements are not arbitrary and that it doesn't "guide the licensee along the path of programming." [7]

These same controls could not legally be imposed on the print media. To counter such criticism, the Commission acknowledges that broadcast media are different from print media; they come into the American living room in full sight or sound of children and the emotionally unstable.[8]

The Commission reiterates that it works within the boundaries of the First Amendment. Does it overstep these boundaries, or are its actions justified, especially as they deal with radio news? For an answer, let's examine the First Amendment.

THE FIRST AMENDMENT

When the founding fathers declared in the First Amendment of the Constitution, "Congress shall make no law. . . abridging the freedom of speech, or of the press. . . ," they set in motion a press less hampered in its operations than any other press in the world. With the emergence of radio, suddenly there was a new "press" upon the scene. How would the

---

[4] Sydney W. Head, *Broadcasting In America: A Survey of Television and Radio,* 3rd ed. (Boston: Houghton Mifflin Company, 1976), p. 345.
[5] *Report and Statement of Policy re: Commission en banc Programming Inquiry,* FCC 60-970, July 29, 1960.
[6] See: Federal Communications Commission, *Public Service Responsibility of Broadcast Licensees: The Blue Book,* March 7, 1946, Part III C., "Discussion of Public Issues."
[7] See: *Report and Statement of Policy re: Commission en banc Programming Inquiry,* FCC 60-970, July 29, 1960.
[8] *Ibid.*

courts judge the actions of this new press as compared to the print medium? The Supreme Court has decreed that the broadcast media are afforded protection equal to their print media counterparts under the First Amendment. In the 1948 Supreme Court case of the *U.S.* v. *Paramount Pictures,* the court stated, ". . . moving pictures, like newspapers and radio, are included in the press, whose freedom is guaranteed by the First Amendment." [9] Supreme Court Justice William O. Douglas said in the 1954 case of *Superior Films* v. *Department of Education* that, ". . . the First Amendment draws no distinction between the various methods of communicating ideas." [10] In 1959, the Supreme Court repeated this stance in the case of *Farmer's Education and Cooperative Union* v. *WDAY, Inc.,* by declaring, ". . . expressly applying this country's tradition of free expression to the field of radio broadcasting, Congress has from the first emphatically forbidden the Commission to exercise any power of censorship over radio communication." [11]

This First Amendment protection is equal, but it's nevertheless separate. This feeling was expressed in 1966 by Justice Burger when he said:

> A broadcaster has much in common with a newspaper publisher, but he is not in the same category in terms of public obligations imposed by law. A broadcaster seeks and is granted the free and exclusive use of a limited and valuable part of the public domain; when he accepts that franchise it is burdened by enforceable public obligations. A newspaper can be operated at the whim or caprice of its owners; a broadcast station cannot.[12]

Are these "enforceable" public obligations that Justice Burger refers to Constitutional? The Supreme Court has apparently decided that they are, due to the limited number of radio frequencies. In its 1943 case, *National Broadcasting Co.* v. *United States,* the Court declared:

> Unlike other media of expression, radio inherently is not available to all. That is its unique characteristic; and that is why, unlike other modes of expression, it is subject to government regulation. Because it cannot be used by all, some who wish to use it must be denied. . . The standard provided for the licensing of stations by the Communications Act of 1934 was the "public interest, convenience, or necessity."

[9] *United States* v. *Paramount Pictures,* 334 U.S. 131, 92 L.Ed. 1260, 68 S. Ct. 915 (1948).
[10] *Superior Films* v. *Department of Education,* 346 U.S. 587 (1954).
[11] *Farmer's Educational and Cooperative Union of America, North Dakota Division* v. *WDAY, Inc.,* 360 U.S. 525, 3 L.Ed. 2d 1407, 79 S. Ct. 1302 (1959).
[12] *Office of Communication of United Church of Christ* v. *F.C.C.,* 123 U.S. App. D. C. 328, 359 F. 2d 994, 1003 (D.C. Cir. 1966).

Denial of a station license on that ground, if valid under the Act, is not a denial of free speech.[13]

THE FAIRNESS DOCTRINE

With the legal foundation for control of radio thus firmly established, we come to another important document that has a direct effect on radio news, the Fairness Doctrine. The FCC's Fairness Doctrine is basically concerned with access to the media for the free expression of public issues. With direct reference to news programming, the Doctrine states that:

A licensee would be abusing his position as public trustee of these important means of mass communication were he to withhold from expression over his facilities relevant news or facts concerning a controversy or to slant or distort the presentation of such news.[14]

The key to the wording of the Doctrine is its deliberate lack of reference to a specific newscast. Thus, the licensee, and you as a radio journalist, are protected under the First Amendment when it comes to airing, say, the 8:00 A.M. news. However, if, over a period of a week or longer, you deliberately slanted the news toward a given issue, and it could be proven, then there would be the danger of serious repercussions. Thus, although not the licensee of the station, you do have a responsibility for the license when it comes to the fair presentation of news in your community. Remember, it is the overall posture of your station's total news programming that the Fairness Doctrine applies to, not just a specific newscast.

The Doctrine has similar guidelines that apply to editorial comment. In 1941, the FCC decided that broadcasting stations should not air editorials, saying in its Mayflower Decision, "A truly free radio cannot be used to advocate the causes of the licensee." [15] However, in 1949, the Commission reversed that policy when it issued the Fairness Doctrine, stating that stations do have the right to editorialize if they "provide a reasonable amount of time . . . for the expression of the contrasting views of all the responsible elements in the community on the various issues which arise . . ." [16] The Doctrine doesn't require stations to provide "equal" time for reply to the editorials on any issue, but it does stress that an "ap-

---

[13] *National Broadcasting Co.* v. *United States, Columbia Broadcasting System, Inc.* v. *Same,* 319 U.S. 190, 87 L.Ed. 1344, 63 S.Ct. 997 (1943).

[14] Federal Communications Commission, *In The Matter of Editorializing by Broadcast Licensees: The Fairness Doctrine,* 13 FCC 1246 (June 1, 1949), p. 17.

[15] *In the Matter of the Mayflower Broadcasting Corporation and The Yankee Network, Inc. (WAAB),* 8 FCC 333, 338 (January 16, 1941).

[16] *In the Matter of Editorializing . . . The Fairness Doctrine.*

proximate" amount of time should be provided, and that the reply should air before an approximately equal audience. For example, if your station's editorial aired during the peak drive-time hour of 5:00 P.M., when scores of listeners tune in, then a reply to that editorial should also be aired during a drive-time period. Also, if your station's editorial lasted fifteen minutes, a thirty-second reply would not be fair.

Noncommercial educational broadcasting stations, however, are prohibited from editorializing. Congress made this the law of the land when its Public Broadcasting Act of 1967 amended Section 399(a) of the Communications Act of 1934.

Again you may ask, "Are all of these restrictions Constitutional under the First Amendment?" Apparently so, declared the courts in the 1967 case, *Red Lion Broadcasting Co. v. Federal Communications Commission.*[17] This case dealt with what is called the Fairness Doctrine's "personal attack" rule. Under this rule, when an individual is personally "attacked" on the air, the station airing the attack must give that individual an opportunity to reply. This rule and the Fairness Doctrine itself were challenged in the Red Lion case, on the grounds that this restricted the licensee's freedom of expression and added the fear of subsequent punishment through the danger of threat of the loss of the broadcasting license. However, the federal court upheld the Fairness Doctrine due to the unique character of broadcasting airwaves, which are limited and therefore in the public domain. Interestingly enough, in an affirmation of the print media's freedom from regulation, the Supreme Court ruled that a Florida law permitting a political candidate the right of reply to a newspaper criticism of him or her was unconstitutional![18]

The Fairness Doctrine is not a law, only an official statement from a Commission designated by Congress to regulate broadcasting. The Commission nevertheless considers, "strict adherence" to it "as the single most important requirement . . . for grant of a renewal license."[19]

After increased pressure from the broadcasting industry over the ban of cigarette commercials, the FCC issued the "Fairness Report" in 1974 to examine the Doctrine's history and clarify certain issues for broadcasters. It removed a ruling it had inserted into the Doctrine in 1967 requiring that cigarette commercials be countered by antismoking announcements. That 1967 clause had caused numerous problems for broadcasters, who, for example, were receiving requests for antipollution announcements to coun-

---

[17] *Red Lion Broadcasting Co. v. Federal Communications Commission,* 127 U.S. App. D. C. 129, 381 F. 2d 908 (1967).
[18] Had the court upheld the Florida law, speculation was that a federal law on right of reply might have been forthcoming. For a background perspective on the case (*Miami Herald* v. *Tornillo,* 1974), see: *The Quill,* Vol. 62, No. 4 (April, 1974), p. 6.
[19] *Committee for the Fair Broadcasting of Controversial Issues,* 25 FCC 2d 283, 292 (1970).

ter oil corporation commercials. The 1974 Report stated that the cigarette ruling was a departure from the Doctrine's central purpose, which was "to facilitate the development of an informed public opinion." The Report did, however, maintain the constitutionality of the Fairness Doctrine, recognizing "the responsibility of government in maintaining and enhancing a system of freedom of expression." Stressing autonomy of broadcast journalism, the Report reaffirmed the Fairness Doctrine's provisions that matters of access to and handling of specific public issues are best left to the individual stations. At the time of this writing, however, this Report is being appealed to the courts by the National Citizens Committee for Broadcasting. The Doctrine, although not law, has managed to have the thrust of its purpose enforced through Section 315 of the Communications Act, the Section that specifically concerns political broadcasting.

SECTION 315

Congress spelled out regulations for political broadcasting in the Communications Act of 1934 in its Section 315, which states:

> If any licensee shall permit any person who is a legally qualified candidate for any public office to use a broadcasting station, he shall afford equal opportunities to all other such candidates for that office in the use of the broadcasting station. . .[20]

This law does not apply to a legally qualified candidate's appearance on a:

> (1) bona fide newscast, (2) bona fide news interview, (3) a bona fide news documentary (if the appearance of the candidate is incidental to the presentation of the subject or subjects covered by the news documentary), or (4) on-the-spot coverage of bona fide news events (including but not limited to political conventions and activities incidental thereto).[21]

A 1975 ruling by the FCC added presidential press conferences and press conferences of all other candidates for any political office broadcast live in their entirety to this exemption. The FCC also said that a station carrying a debate between two major party candidates for office is no longer required to afford equal time to minor party candidates.

In essence, if your community's mayor has legally declared he's running for re-election, and your station gives him fifteen minutes of air time to

[20] *The Communications Act of 1934.*
[21] *Committee for the Fair Broadcasting of Controversial Issues.*

discuss his candidacy, your station is then required to give every other candidate for mayor fifteen minutes of air time. This applies to primary and general elections and includes candidates running for everything from municipal offices to national offices. Although these specific news programs are exempt from Section 315, its language clearly states that those programs should be fair in their presentations of controversial issues of public importance. Hence, the Fairness Doctrine's influence is felt within Section 315.

As to what creates a "bona fide' news program, the FCC issued a Section 315 Primer in 1966 to clarify some of the complexities of the law. In it, the FCC has advised broadcasters to consider carefully:

1. the format, nature and content of the programs;
2. whether the format, nature and content of the program has changed since its inception and, if so, in what respects;
3. who initiates the programs;
4. who produces and controls the program;
5. when was the program initiated;
6. is the program regularly scheduled,
7. and if the program is regularly scheduled, specify the time and day of the week when it is broadcast.[22]

For example, the FCC favors exemptions in which the news program has been regularly broadcast over a long time versus a new program.[23]

In addition, if you, a radio journalist, decide to run for office, you must either cease your on-air newscasts or allow your opponent(s) air time equivalent to yours. Since Section 315 generates fine-line legal distinctions, any questions you might have regarding its interpretation should be referred to a qualified legal counsel.

FREE PRESS VS. FAIR TRIAL

Two constitutionally guaranteed rights clash head-on in the United States —the freedom of the press guaranteed by the First Amendment and the right to a fair trial guaranteed by the Sixth Amendment. How far does each compromise the other? That is an unresolved dilemma continually examined and re-examined by all levels of the judicial, legislative and executive branches of government.

The free press/fair trial dilemma is by no means a recent development.

---

[22] *Use of Broadcast Facilities by Candidates for Public Office*, 31 Fed. Reg. 6660 Adopted April 27, 1966; Printed May 4, 1966, Ill, "Uses," in general.
[23] *Letter to WIIC*, 33 F.C.C. 2d 629 (1972).

One of the most bizarre examples of this clash came in 1935, when Bruno Hauptmann was tried for the kidnapping and murder of Charles Lindbergh's child. The journalistic "mob" covering the trial turned it into a circus of publicity, prompting the American Bar Association to enact Canon 35 to its Judicial Ethics. Still in effect today although strongly contested by broadcast journalists, it states:

> Proceedings in court should be conducted with fitting dignity and decorum. The taking of photographs in the courtroom during sessions of the court or recesses between sessions, and the broadcasting of court proceedings are calculated to detract from the essential dignity of the proceedings, degrade the court, and create misconceptions with respect thereto in the mind of the public and should not be permitted.[24]

Canon 35 is not a law, per se, and some sections of the country are giving broadcast media access to courtroom proceedings, provided they meet designated requirements, such as a judge's or defendant's consent.

Another free press/fair trial report emerged after the 1963 assassination of President John Kennedy and the massive news media coverage surrounding the alleged assassin, Lee Harvey Oswald. The American Civil Liberties Union said in a report that had Oswald lived, he would have had no opportunity for a fair trial due to this case's publicity. The Advisory Committee on Fair Trial and Free Press of the American Bar Association then issued its famous Reardon Report in 1968. The Reardon Report deals with pretrial and trial information disseminated by news sources, such as attorneys, judges, and law enforcement officials, and seeks to restrict the information that these sources can divulge to journalists. It contains a series of recommendations for these sources as to information they should and should not impart. It recommends withholding such information as an accused's prior criminal record, the existence or contents of a confession, an admission or statement by the accused, the performance of an examination or test or the refusal to take these tests, the identity, testimony, or credibility of prospective witnesses, the possible plea of guilty to the offense charged or a lesser offense, and any opinion as to the accused's guilt or innocence.[25] Attorneys who divulge this information could be reprimanded or even disbarred. If the Report were to become law, journalists could be charged with contempt. Several state bar associations have accepted these recommendations, either wholly or partially.

Since its inception, most of the abuse of this Report has been by attorneys

---

[24] American Bar Association, *Canon 35*, 1937.
[25] "Fair Trial and Free Press: The Reardon Report," *Advisory Committee on Fair Trial and Free Press of the American Bar Association Project on Minimum Standards*, approved by the American Bar Association House of Delegates, Chicago, February 19, 1968, Part I, 1.1.

and law enforcement officials. Some may not have read the document but know it exists and therefore withhold an enormous amount of information from journalists because of it. However, a defendant still has the judicial safeguards of a change of venue, continuance, a mistrial, and special jury instructions to insure his or her right to a fair trial.

Judges may occasionally order gag rules barring publication or broadcast of court proceedings, information divulged from news sources, court sketches, or sometimes the presence of reporters in courtrooms. Are gag rules constitutional? They're usually voided on appeal, but in the meantime you must contend with the judge's order. Gag rules are a serious unresolved problem for radio journalists.

A rule of thumb in covering court procedures is to insist upon your constitutional freedoms to inform your public, but inform them using the utmost fairness and professionalism. Extreme interpretation of either the First or the Sixth Amendments will accomplish nothing. It's only through the magic of compromise that a satisfactory relationship between you and the courts can prosper.

FREEDOM OF INFORMATION LAWS

As a radio journalist, you may encounter the withholding of information by government agencies. What are your rights of access to this information? The federal Freedom of Information Act enacted by Congress in 1967 and amended in 1974 charts such access rules on public information.

In the Act, agencies are to give the public access for inspection and copying to all but the most sensitive federal documents. Under the amendment, the agency has to prove whether or not a particular document is sensitive enough to be kept secret, either for national security reasons, to protect confidential sources, or for another valid reason. The emphasis is upon the words, "must prove," and if a judge decides that the government can't prove the documents are sensitive enough to warrant withholding them, the official responsible for the withholding can be reprimanded, suspended, or dismissed.

When you ask for access to government documents, you don't have to explain why you want them or who you are. Furthermore, an agency must reply to your request within ten working days and can only charge you for actual duplicating costs, instead of the $1.00 per page some agencies were charging for duplication before the Act was amended. If an agency refuses to give you documents, you have the right to appeal this action to the courts.

Most states also have enacted some type of freedom of information law. Such laws, called "open meeting laws," vary from one state to another.

Some may encompass local governmental units, granting access to school board meetings, prohibiting secret executive sessions of governmental boards, and even specifying penalties for violating these laws. Take the time to check your own state statutes in these areas. They'll have a direct effect on your relationships with these agencies.

RIGHT OF PRIVACY

Freedom of information, or "the public's right to know," is countered in some annals of communication law by the "right of privacy." This "right of privacy" came from an 1890 law review article and was consequently determined in 1903 by the Court of Appeals of New York to read, "the claim that a man has the right to pass through this world, if he wills, without having his picture published . . . or his eccentricities commented upon either in handbills, circulars, catalogues, periodicals or newspapers." [26] Most states recognize this right but this recognition varies; so again, double check your own state's precedents on privacy laws.

Generally judicial precedent has held that news about public officials can be broadcast because these people have given up their private life. The same is true for public figures such as well-known motion picture stars. Anything on a public record, such as a police blotter, can be broadcast, as can news of legitimate public interest. However, some sections of the country limit journalists' access to arrest records.[27] Right to privacy applies to such reporting issues as:

1. Intrusion into an individual's seclusion, solitude, or private affairs;
2. Public disclosure of embarrassing facts about an individual;
3. Publicity which places an individual in a false light in the public eye;
4. Appropriation for the defendant's advantage, of the plaintiff's name or likeness.[28]

In 1974, Congress passed the Privacy Act of 1974, designed basically to protect people from the government abusing information it had compiled about them or indiscriminately disclosing that information outside the government. If a government employee leaks this information, he or she could be fired. News sources could substantially dry up as a result of

[26] *Roberson* v. *Rochester Folding Box Co.,* 171 N.Y., at 544, 64 N.E., at 443.
[27] Lyle Denniston, "A Citizen's Right to Privacy: The Issue Remains Nebulous," *The Quill,* Vol. 63, No. 4 (April, 1975), pp. 16. 19.
[28] Donald Gillmor and Jerome A. Barron, *Mass Communication Law,* 2nd ed. (St. Paul, Minnesota: West Publishing Co., 1974), pp. 287-288.

this Act, and you should carefully monitor future court rulings dealing with this ruling. The Freedom of Information Law and the Privacy Act will inevitably clash over such issues.

If at any time you question whether or not to broadcast a particular news item, consult legal counsel.

LIBEL

When reporting with right of privacy in mind, also keep in mind the definition of libel. A standard definition of libel is "any false statement, written or broadcast, which tends to: (1) Bring any person into public hatred, contempt or ridicule, or (2) Cause him to be shunned or avoided, or (3) Injure him in his business or profession." [29] Libel is not a crime but rather a *tort,* which is a civil wrong in which an individual brings an action to court because of supposed damages done to him or her. What is libelous in one section of the country may not be libelous somewhere else; what might have been libelous in the 1930s may not be libelous now; and what might be libelous in one instance may not be under a different set of circumstances.

Libel arises in two forms: libel per se, which is defamation at face value of the words, but under which the Supreme Court requires that an injured person additionally prove "intentional or reckless falsehood or negligence;" and libel per quod, which is indirect defamation because of association or special circumstances, under which the person would have to prove that your broadcast was damaging.[30] These two forms create some hazy legal distinctions. Generally, libel per se can include such words and phrases as communist, incompetent, degenerate, corrupt, fascist, drug addict, and bigamist.

Libelous broadcasts come from careless reporting. You're in a hurry. Your next newscast is ten minutes away. You can't reach your news source to verify a report. The report says that a man named John Doe has been taken into custody on charges of embezzling $5,000 to pay off a gambling debt. You decide to broadcast that information, identifying John Doe by name in the report. By the time your newscast is over, your station manager has received a stinging phone call from John Doe's lawyer saying that the station libeled his client, and that he is suing the station. Why? The accused embezzler's name was John Doer, not John Doe. You, as a radio journalist,

[29] Jerome L. Nelson, *Libel* (Ames, Iowa: Iowa State University Press, 1973), p. 3. Quoting from: Paul P. Ashley, *Say It Safely* (Seattle, Washington: U. of Washington Press, 1966).

[30] For a review of the current status of libel statutes, see: D. Charles Whitney, "Libel: New Ground Rules for an Old Ball Game," *The Quill,* Vol. 62, No. 8 (August, 1974), pp. 22-25.

have carelessly committed the three sins that add up to actionable libel: you've *defamed* the person by injuring his reputation, you've *identified* him, and you've *published* or broadcast that defamation. As it is, unless you and your radio station can show truth, qualified privilege (a news medium broadcasting a fair report of public proceedings), or fair comment (because the issue invited public controversy), you may be subject to paying a large claim for damages. If your station broadcasts a complete and quick apology and retraction of the news story, it might help your case but it won't assure you protection from a suit.

Corporations can also sue if you've broadcast a statement questioning their credit rating, disparaging their honesty, or charging them with fraud or mismanagement.[31] It is considered safe to say that a person has made a mistake, since courts agree that everyone makes mistakes. Since personal privileges are extended to corporations, this rule applies to them also. Along this line, unions can sue if they feel their reputations have been defamed, that reputation being a common property of the union members.[32]

You can, however, freely criticize governmental bodies and municipal corporations. Certainly erroneous criticism based on untruths is unwarranted and unprofessional, but you do have the right to criticize such bodies. Remember, you still have the defenses of truth, qualified privilege, and fair comment.

Picking up a defamation by another medium and rebroadcasting it also puts you in jeopardy of libel. Even if you attribute defamation to an identified medium, you can still be sued for damages.[33]

Journalists do have some legal safeguards concerning libel. A public official or a public figure must prove actual malice on an issue of public interest or concern, or deliberate broadcast of a statement knowing it was false, or reckless disregard for the truth. Private citizens used to be included in this category but were removed in a 1974 Supreme Court ruling. Private citizens consequently must prove fault or negligence, and each state is allowed to define "negligence."

SHIELD LAWS

One area of reporting, the protection of the confidentiality of news sources, has not clearly come under the First Amendment protection. In the 1972 Branzburg decision, the Supreme Court declared that journalists

---

[31] Gilmor and Barron, p. 188.
[32] *Daniels* v. *Sanitarium Ass'n Inc.,* 30 Cal. Rptr. 828, 381 P. 2d 652 (1963); *Kelley* v. *New York Herald Tribune, Inc.,* 175 N.Y. S 2d 598 (1958).
[33] *Maloof* v. *Post Publishing Co.,* 306 Mass. 279, 28 N.E. 2d 458 (1940).

must respond to grand jury subpoenas and questions requesting them to divulge their confidential news sources before such juries.[34] If you refuse to divulge your confidential news sources, you can be held in contempt of court and face fines, imprisonment, or both. Although you may win your case if appealed, you can spend some interim time behind bars.

Realizing this, many states have passed legislation aimed at protecting the confidentiality of news sources. This legislation is commonly called *shield laws*. These shield laws vary from state to state in their degree of protection, and you should become familiar with your own state's current law, if it has enacted one. For example, in Indiana before 1973 only *commercially* licensed radio and television stations were protected by the Indiana shield law. When the shield law was amended, the word "commercially" was deleted, thus incorporating all employees of educational radio stations in Indiana into the shield law's protection. Furthermore, Indiana shield law protects information that is either broadcast or not broadcast by a radio or television station. That means that reporter's notes or part of an audio actuality that was not aired are protected in Indiana. In other states it may not be. The original Indiana shield law required that reporters receive their principal income from the practice of reporting. The 1973 amendment eliminated the word "principal," with the result that part-time journalists also came under the shield law's protection.

If your state does have a reporter's shield law, study it. It is important for you to be aware of it and understand it. A review of the history of your state's shield law and the court cases that have challenged its validity or reaffirmed its constitutionality will also help you. In addition, familiarize yourself with the language and court challenges of neighboring states' shield laws. In some instances, a court in another state may rule differently from a court in your state, even though the language of the two shield laws are basically the same. The phrase "forewarned is forearmed" applies here, especially if your broadcast reaches across state boundaries.

SELF-REGULATION

To discourage the encroachment of government regulations on broadcasting, the industry has established and encouraged self-regulation, mainly through the various professional journalism and broadcasting associations.

[34] For a perspective on related Supreme Court decisions see: Tom Dorris, "The Supreme Court Rules," *The Quill,* Vol. 62, No. 8 (August, 1974), p. 20.

One such organization is the *National Association of Broadcasters*. It was organized in 1922 as a nonprofit association to, among other things, foster the development of broadcasting, protect members from injustices, and "do all things necessary and proper to encourage and promote customs and practices which will strengthen and maintain" the industry. Through a Board of Directors elected by its members, the NAB lobbies before Congress and other government agencies. It has established a Radio Code to define programming standards, including those for radio news. The Code stresses that radio journalists should carefully select reliable news sources; that they should be factual, objective, and diligent in reporting; and that they should exercise ethical judgment in covering news and public events. Adherence to these guidelines is voluntary for NAB members.

Founded in 1909, the *Society of Professional Journalists, Sigma Delta Chi,* is another professional organization. It too has established a code of ethics for its members dealing with responsibility, freedom of the press, ethics, accuracy, and objectivity.

The *Radio/Television News Directors Association (RTNDA)* is an organization of radio and television news directors that also has a code of news ethics. RTNDA's code states that the broadcast journalists' primary purpose is to inform people of important and interesting events as accurately and comprehensively as possible.

Other professional communications organizations, such as *Women In Communication, Inc.* and *American Women in Radio and Television, Inc.,* also have creeds their members follow.

Although codes established by associations are important, they are only as good as their membership wants them to be. These associations have very limited enforcement powers. Even in the NAB, enforcement is mostly concerned with the type and amount of commercial messages aired on member stations. Some associations assess special fees for belonging to their "code," and this policy has come under fire from some members. Nevertheless, definite advantages lie in membership in professional associations, especially for people working in radio news. Many radio stations are located in relatively small markets, and the news staff may consist of only one or two reporters. Association with other working professionals through such membership helps keep radio journalists from being isolated from their profession, its goals, and its responsibilities.

The Code of Broadcast News Ethics of RTNDA, the news section from the NAB Radio Code, and the Code of Ethics of the Society of Professional Journalists, Sigma Delta Chi, are found in the Appendix at the end of this book.

SUMMARY

Chapter 8 dealt with the regulation of radio journalism and its recent history. Guided by the realization that the airwaves are limited, the FCC emerged to regulate the airwaves in the public's interest, convenience, and necessity. The First Amendment, which guarantees freedom of the press, has been interpreted by the courts to also protect freedom of the radio press, prohibiting the FCC from regulating radio journalism. Nevertheless, radio is still in some ways considered to be "separate" from the print media. For example, the FCC enacted the Fairness Doctrine, stating that stations must provide time for reply to controversial issues voiced on that station. Section 315 of the Communications Act also took the "separate" press view, and declared that all political candidates must be offered equal time for political broadcasts.

Other regulations and codes deal with the free press/fair trial dilemma, with regulations barring tape recorders from courtrooms, prohibiting news sources from revealing trial information, and sometimes even preventing reporters from entering courtrooms. On the side of deregulation, the freedom of information laws at both the national and state levels give citizens and reporters access to most government documents. However, this "right to know" is countered in some instances by a person's "right of privacy." Libel is another area of regulation and encompasses false statements you may broadcast. Still other regulations, shield laws, protect journalists and the confidentiality of their news sources.

Finally, regulation takes on a self-governing aspect in the form of professional journalism and broadcasting organizations and their codes of ethics. The professional organizations, however, are only as strong as their members' support.

SUGGESTED EXERCISES

1. Does your state or a nearby state have a reporters' shield law or a freedom of information law? What are their provisions?
2. The district executive of your local phone company is running for mayor. He's also this year's United Way director for your city. You air his voice reporting the latest local fund drive contributions on your noon newscast. Your station receives a call from another mayoral candidate, who heard the newscast and is demanding equal time. Are you required to honor this request? Why?

3. You discover documented information that one of your state's senators has apparently paid an incredibly low personal income tax, and that something looks amiss. After thoroughly checking this information for accuracy, your news team decides to broadcast this news. The senator sues your station for libel. What defenses do you have?

4. You want to take your tape recorder into the city court to record some of the proceedings of a controversial murder trial. The judge says you're welcome to report the trial, but your tape recorder will have to remain behind. Upon what is the judge basing his decision?

5. You comply with the city judge's order not to take your tape recorder into the courtroom, but want to know if the defendant has taken a lie detector test or not. When you ask the police officer in charge, he says, "No comment." Upon what is the officer basing his silence?

ANNOUNCEMENTS

	60 Sec	30 Sec
1	9.00	6.50
52	6.50	5.50
156	6.00	5.00
312	5.00	4.00
624	4.50	3.50
1040	3.50	2.50

chapter nine

Promotion and Sales

Promotion and sales go hand in hand in any business, and the business of broadcasting is no exception. News contributes to the success of that business by providing broadcasting with a promotable and saleable product. This in no way says that news should be pandered or that commercial sponsorship need be its ultimate goal. Like other businesses, broadcasting needs to maintain its visibility to the public. Promotional activities are one way of achieving this visibility. This chapter will cover some of the reasons for developing promotional activities, types of activities available to stations, and effective use of them.

PROMOTION FOR A PURPOSE

The degree to which stations promote their news departments to the public depends primarily on two factors: market size and competition. Promotion is usually more intense in larger markets than in smaller ones because it normally takes more effort to be visible amidst the increased competition of more radio stations. Directly related to market size is competition. If one station heavily promotes its news department, then the other stations in that market will also find it necessary to increase their promotional activities.

Reasons to Promote

Reasons to promote a station and its news department vary. Some stations have a large promotion budget with a special department and staff to handle these activities exclusively. For the most part, the reasons will fall into seven areas, all geared toward enhancing the image of the station in the community, and ultimately improving commercial sponsorship.

Ownership change. When a new owner or manager assumes responsibility at a station, he or she naturally wants to do everything possible to assure the success of this new business venture. Therefore, new owners or managers will usually mount a promotional campaign to show the listeners, advertisers, and competing stations that they're making an impact on the market.

Ratings. When broadcast rating organizations enter a market to measure listenership, the stations naturally want to end up with a good showing. They may help to insure this by increasing their promotional activities during the rating period. However, to safeguard against measuring a "false" rating for a station that only garners a high listenership because of this increased promotional activity, the rating organizations will note in their report that the station participated in promotion during the rating period. We'll examine ratings in more detail later in this chapter.

Format change. A change in a station's musical format may also cause a change in the news format. As discussed in Chapter 7, a contemporary music station normally incorporates a fairly short newscast. When a format change occurs, the station will usually promote it.

Seniority and the newcomer. Stations known for their news coverage and seniority in their market may use their reputation as a basis for promotion. For example, a station celebrating its twenty-fifth anniversary of broadcasting will usually develop a promotion associated with this anniversary. Stations wishing to enhance their news department's image and gain an edge on their competition may seek occasions for such a promotional campaign.

New call letters. When a station changes its call letters, perhaps through a change of ownership or a management decision, it needs to promote the new call letters and capitalize upon this new visibility.

Seasonal promotion. In a college or university town or resort community where there is a transient population, the station needs to develop a promotional campaign each time this new population arrives.

New equipment. The addition of new equipment also lends itself to a promotional campaign. For example, a change in the color scheme of a mobile news unit or the addition of a helicopter to aid in news gathering are both opportunities for promotion.

All of the above factors play an important part in the decision to develop promotional campaigns for the news department. Once such a decision has been made, the next step is to decide what type of promotion would be best and how to implement it.

Award-Winning News

Of all promotional activities, the most important one is promoting the fact that your station's news team has won an award or received an honor or citation. When this happens, station management will usually publicize the event to both the listeners and the business community.

Radio journalists rarely receive feedback about the quality of their work, even though they may communicate with thousands of people every day. People are in the habit of writing letters to newspapers, not radio stations. When they have a complaint, they simply turn the dial; when they are pleased or interested, they usually just keep listening. Thus, winning an award may be the only feedback a radio reporter receives. But more significantly, awards provide recognition and satisfaction for the reporter, the news department, and the station.

The decision to seek a radio news award must be a team effort rather than an ego trip for a chosen few. When the decision is made, all members of the news team should participate in the competition. When the award is won, everyone can share the satisfaction.

Small market stations or less recognized stations in larger markets may feel they are out of the running when it comes to news awards. This is a fallacy. Opportunities abound for everyone to participate. The key is to seek out the awards you want to win and determine how best to compete for them. Your own community has many opportunities for awards in press association or press club competition. State press associations, especially those connected with the wire services, usually offer an awards competition. Many of these are designed by categories so that a small market radio station with a small news staff will not find itself competing with a huge metropolitan news force. Such professional associations as the Radio-Television News Directors Association and the Society of Professional Journalists, Sigma Delta Chi have well established and prestigious radio news awards. Other prestigious national news awards sought after by radio journalists include the George Peabody Awards for Radio and Television, The American Bar Association "Gavel Awards," the Armstrong Awards for Excellence in FM Broadcasting, and The National Headliner Awards.

Once you've decided to seek awards, you'll need a definite plan to compete effectively. First, you'll need to obtain a list of awards for which your news department may be eligible. Write the National Association of Broadcasters in Washington or check the awards deadline listings which appear periodically in the calendar of events in *Broadcasting* magazine. When you receive this information, the next step is to develop an entry.

Check through the station's news files for a possible entry. Some news programs that are suitable for a particular award may have been saved on tape. If you can't find a suitable entry on file, then you'll need to prepare one. There is one important consideration. You must determine if seeking awards will disrupt the priorities of your news department. Obviously, if news personnel concentrate solely on awards competition and ignore their daily reporting efforts, then the competition is a process of diminishing returns.

Another necessary part of competing for news awards is to establish a task flow chart to schedule your efforts toward the award deadline. For example, suppose you have decided to do a medical care documentary to enter in national competition, and the deadline for entries is December 31. You've determined that your community will benefit from such a program and you plan to produce it. The flow chart will provide you with a schedule of dates for completion of each phase of documentary production—research, interviews, writing, production, and editing. A series of deadlines scheduled well in advance of the entry deadline will suffice as a good flow chart. In larger news departments, you may want to assign specific people to handle each phase of the production.

Publicizing Awards

Once you've captured a news award, your station's management will want to publicize it. Publicizing an award is beneficial for many reasons: it can trigger a sudden interest in commercial sponsorship of newscasts; it can give your station "award-winning" prestige, which can be reflected in its credibility as well as its ratings; it can also boost the morale of the news department.

Television. Television is one way to advertise the fact you've won an award. One of the best positions to place the advertising is adjacent to the television newscasts. The same audience that tunes to the evening television newscast is also likely to tune to a radio newscast during the day.

Newspaper. The newspaper gives you the advantages of a true local medium. Thus, your publicity can take a hometown approach. Like television, you're again reaching an audience interested in news who may not be regular listeners to your station.

Billboards. Billboards also serve a mass audience, only at a much lower cost per thousand persons reached than television. It's also the audience that listens to car radios. Thus, it's another ideal medium for advertising your news awards. If your station has a visual *logo* (identifying symbol) or theme, this can be used in the television, newspaper, and billboard advertisements, constantly reinforcing your "award-winning" promotion.

Trade publications. Advertising your news awards in trade magazines has two advantages. First, it can increase the prestige and image of the station among other broadcasters. Second, such ads reach advertising agencies and increase the chances of the agency placing commercials on your station. That can translate into more revenue for your news department.

Direct mail. Direct mail is the most specialized and personal medium. With a list obtained from direct mail companies or your own phone book, you can specify the exact people or institutions you wish your publicity to reach. This process is the most expensive per thousands of persons reached, but does not waste any of your advertising dollars. A very effective direct mail approach to advertise your news award is to print a pamphlet and insert it in the station's monthly billings. You can also send these pamphlets to advertising agencies throughout the country and to organizations like the Chamber of Commerce, who can tuck them into promotional packets for new businesses in your community.

Your own station. One of the best and least expensive places to publicize your news awards is on your own station. The most common method is to promote the awards in the intros and outros of regularly scheduled newscasts. For example, a newscast might begin:

AND NOW FOR THE AWARD-WINNING NEWS TEAM, HERE IS JOHN DOE . . .

Another variation of this might read:

WAZY AWARD-WINNING NEWS IS BROUGHT TO YOU BY . . .

The decision to advertise any facet of radio news should be made jointly by management and news personnel. Some stations may have specific budgets for promotion and advertising, and the news department can take part in planning these budget expenditures. The next decision is to determine what type of advertising will be the most effective.

The Ratings

As discussed earlier, stations can subscribe to various broadcast rating services to determine how they measure up in comparison to other stations in their markets. The American Research Bureau (ARB) is one of many.

There are as many opinions about the effectiveness of rating services as there are services. Every service claims to be the most reliable and accurate. Except in information or all-news formats, rating services do not play an exceptionally large part in the news department's operation because rating services do not fully reflect the news department's total impact on its community. Also, the rating service usually concentrates on musical programming. Thus, decisions that affect the news department should not be based solely on ratings. When news programming specifically shows a low rating, it is wise to review such factors as individual newscasters, the competition, and the type or amount of coverage given to specific areas of the city to determine whether you can strengthen these ratings. When the ratings do go up, this can be promoted, especially to the business community and potential advertisers.

Professional Involvement

Another means of promoting your station's news team is through professional involvement of the news staff. An advantage of professional involvement is that it extends the image of your station beyond the parameters of its listenership. One of the best ways to do this is through your membership in professional associations.

State and metropolitan press associations. All states have state press associations. These may be state broadcasters' associations, state news directors', or journalists' associations. Some larger cities have metropolitan press clubs. Usually the two wire services, AP and UPI, have professional associations in every state, and all radio reporters whose stations subscribe to the services are invited to join their respective state organizations.

Radio-Television News Directors Association (RTNDA). The membership of RTNDA is comprised of people actively involved in either directing a station's news department or directing news personnel. The association does provide a substantial voice for national broadcast journalists.

Society of Professional Journalists, Sigma Delta Chi. This association is open to all broadcast and print journalists who are actively engaged in the news process. Recent amendments to the constitution of the association also permit those involved in certain allied media fields to be members of the organization. Founded in 1909, it has continued to grow substantially over the past half century. The association is one of the strongest voices representing all practicing journalists and takes an active role in issues affecting the profession. Many regional as well as educational chapters are located throughout the United States.

National Association of Broadcasters (NAB). NAB is the largest broadcasting organization and one of the major voices that represents the industry. Radio journalists from NAB stations can participate in NAB conventions and regional seminars.

National Association of Educational Broadcasters (NAEB). For those involved in news operations of educational stations, the NAEB provides an opportunity for fellowship with other educational broadcasters. Annual meetings and special workshops and seminars provide an opportunity to interact with professionals in all fields of educational broadcasting.

Broadcast Education Association (BEA). BEA differs from NAEB in that BEA is more concerned with broadcast education. The association usually meets annually in conjunction with the NAB and also sponsors some regional meetings, which provide an opportunity for those involved in radio journalism education to meet with fellow teachers.

Asociation for Education in Journalism (AEJ). AEJ is also comprised of journalism educators. Much like BEA, AEJ enables radio journalism educators to meet not only with other broadcast journalism teachers but also with those involved in print journalism instruction.

Women in Communication, Inc. (WICI). WICI is an organization comprised mostly of women who are actively engaged in a field of communication, although men are also eligible for membership. This includes journalists, public relations and advertising people in both print and broadcast media, as well as communication educators.

American Women in Radio and Television. Consisting of professional women in all areas of broadcasting, the organization permits radio journalists to meet annually with fellow professionals and station management.

International Communication Association. The membership consists primarily of academicians and professionals interested in various aspects of communication theory and research.

Civic Involvement

Active involvement in civic organizations cannot increase your station's visibility. Along with increasing your awareness of community issues and concerns, such involvement can promote the impact of the station in the community, especially since members of the organization are themselves radio listeners.

Organizations to which news personnel can belong include such service organizations as the Lions, Rotary, Kiwanis, Elks, and Shriners. Charitable organizations include the American Cancer Society, Red Cross, United Way, Boy Scouts, Girls Scouts, and similar organizations.

Many times media representatives, especially broadcasters, are requested by organizations to act as announcers or masters of ceremonies for community events. If invited to take part in these activities, you should welcome the opportunity. Again, besides serving your community, you are also promoting your news department.

SELLING RADIO NEWS

There is a definite reason to discuss sales in a radio journalism text. Every radio station—aside from educational stations, which operate on fixed appropriations—must make a profit to stay in business. This is a fact of American journalism that permeates all media.

The Sales Staff

The sales staff is the key to any station's livelihood. These individuals are responsible for bringing income into the station that ultimately pays your salary. A close working relationship between the news and sales departments can be beneficial to both. At some stations, a barrier seems to exist between the two, based on the old tradition that commercialism has no place in good journalism—which it hasn't. However, an awareness and understanding of the functions of both news and sales can aid in achieving maximum benefit for the station.

Account executives know that to be effective, they must be enthusiastic about their product. Much of the responsibility for generating this enthusiasm rests with the news department. You should keep the sales department informed of special activities or awards you receive and pass along to them any complimentary letters from listeners, business, or civil organizations as tangible evidence of the news department's impact on the community.

Sales Prospectus

The news department may also find it helpful to prepare a sales prospectus. An easy way is to purchase a sharp-looking loose-leaf notebook with clear plastic inserts to present a visual image of your news department's activities. The sales staff can then use it to explain the news department to potential sponsors. Your first notebook page could be a letter from the news director explaining the news philosophy of the station. The second page could display pictures of the news staff, while the third page could display pictures of the news studios. An effective fourth page could contain a picture of the mobile news unit or other equipment. Additional notebook pages could show sample daily news schedules and complimentary letters from listeners. The sales prospectus can become as sophisticated, elaborate, and expensive as your news department and station desire. Whatever type of prospectus you create, it can be a valuable sales tool and can help spawn a closer working relationship between the sales and news departments.

News Sponsorship

Radio news has distinct advantages for advertisers unmatched by other radio programming. The first advantage is that news develops a very attentive listenership. Dr. Ernest Dichter, President of the Institute for Motivational Research, describes news as eliciting a "special atmosphere of concentration and alertness" from its listeners. When studies show that the individual consumer is bombarded with approximately three hundred advertisements of all types per day, the advertiser must devise some means to attract the consumer's attention and comprehension. When the advertiser finds a ready-made attentive audience, half the battle is won. Radio news and information are prime examples of "foreground" programming, versus musical "background" programming. The news format intrusively commands attention—a perfect setting for impact and retention of commercial messages. A study by Motivational Analysis Incorporated showed that the attention/retention level of radio listeners was a resounding 65 percent for the news, as compared to its nearest competitor, middle of the road music, at 45 percent.[1]

A second advantage for news is that it's a credible and reputable type of programming and therefore an ideal one for a credible and reputable business to sponsor. For example, an electric and gas company has sponsored the morning network news report on one radio station for twenty years. On another station, a leading bank has sponsored the early morning local news for fifteen years, a regional supermarket chain has sponsored the late morning news for eight years, and a national automotive firm has sponsored the weekend news on a co-operative basis with its local automotive outlet for ten years. Thus, news sponsorship can almost become a tradition. Newscasters themselves enjoy considerable prestige, and this adds to the credibility and prestige of the sponsor.

The third distinct advantage is the type of person that listens to a radio newscast. A study conducted by all-news radio WCBS in New York City found basic characteristics in the male listeners of radio news. First, the study showed that more than one-fourth of the men who tuned to WCBS during an average week were reported to have a personal income of $15,000 or more per year. This incidence of top-income males in the WCBS radio audience was 41 percent above the New York City market

[1] "Study of Attention Levels by Format," Motivational Analysis Incorporated, 1965.

average. Second, the study showed more than one out of every three weekly WCBS male listeners fell into the professional/managerial occupation category. From an advertising standpoint, such a person has an above-average buying power and a highly acquisitive lifestyle. When compared to the rest of the New York market, the WCBS top-occupation male audience was 56 percent above the market average. Third, more than 40 percent of that audience could be classified as white collar workers, which was 32 percent above the New York City market average. Fourth, more than one-fifth of the men who listened to WCBS during an average week were college graduates. Again, this characteristic registered 56 percent higher than the market average of male college graduates.[2]

Another study, conducted by the Brand Rating Index, researched the female as well as the male population and found that the percentage of women from $15,000+ annual income households who listened to a radio news format placed second only to the "good music" radio format.[3]

Radio news sponsorship also permits advertisers to purchase a "fixed time" announcement, specifying which time of day they wish their commercials to be aired. This arrangement also enables the advertiser to have the commercial rotated over a given week. For example, a firm may want to purchase ten commercials in the news per week, two per day. On Monday, the two commercials could air in the morning news at 7:00 A.M.; on Tuesday, they could air in the noon news; on Wednesday, they could air on the 5:00 P.M. news; and on Thursday, they could return to the 7:00 A.M. news. Notice how this rotation format permits total penetration into each time period in any week. Furthermore, it caters to the life styles of all individuals in the market, from the morning or evening commuter to the afternoon homemaker. Other sponsorship combinations are possible through advertising on stations with twenty-four separate daily newscasts, permitting total saturation of a market and almost unlimited rotation combinations.

These are just some of the advantages, characteristics, and aspects of selling radio news. Although the successful financial operation of any radio news department is closely allied to the effectiveness of the station's sales department, news should in no way be prostituted to gain commercial sponsorship, and this should be clearly understood by both the sales and news department. These two departments should not and can not be diametrically opposed to each other if the station is to be a viable force in the community. Certainly it's awkward for the radio journalist to discover that the president of the corporation that sponsors the noon news has been indicted on a

2 "Newsradio and Men," WCBS Newsradio 88, New York, 1972.
3 *Format Book,* Brand Rating Index, 1969. The actual study placed news at 19.8 percent of all female listeners 18+ years of age, and "good music" at 23.6 percent of that same audience. n.d.

bribery charge. Nevertheless, this fact must be reported as news. But an awareness of the importance of sales promotion can move the news department from the losing column into the profit column for management. This trend can only help, not hinder, the increased professionalism of radio journalism.

SUMMARY

Promotion and sales are vital to radio news. To increase a station's visibility among its audience, the news team can develop promotional activities around various themes. These promotional themes can include your station's news awards or the strength of your station's news ratings as compared to other stations. Becoming active in various professional and civic organizations is another excellent way to increase your station's visibility.

Selling radio news is an economic fact of life, and news is a unique saleable commodity. It can gain and retain listeners at a high level of concentration, which is a "must" for advertisers. Consequently, cooperation between your station's sales force and news team is vital to the excellence of the station.

SUGGESTED EXERCISES

1. Write for a free copy of the radio news awards booklet from the National Association of Broadcasters, 1771 N Street, N.W., Washington, D. C., 20036. Determine those awards for which you are eligible to compete.

2. What entry could you use to enter each of these awards competitions? Provide a theme and the information you would include in your entry.

3. Make up a sample flow chart for a radio documentary.

4. Talk to the manager or media buyer of a local advertising agency or of an advertising department in a local firm. Find out when and to what client they would recommend purchasing commercial air time on a radio news program, and why.

5. Interview the manager of a local bank for his or her views about advertising on a radio news program.

chapter ten

Landing a Job

The purpose of this chapter is to assist you in obtaining a job. It is written for the student still in school who is interested in a career in radio journalism. It will also prove useful to people in the industry who want to change jobs or people in allied fields who want to enter the profession. If for some reason you have turned to this chapter first without reading the rest of the book, you're off to a bad start. Radio is a unique medium. It cannot be compared to newspapers or television. Radio people think differently, they work differently, and their medium reflects this difference. Compared to newspaper or television journalists, the radio journalist writes differently, rewrites differently, and uses sound differently. So, if you're just starting this book, stop here and read Chapters 1 through 9 first. If you've already read the earlier chapters, then let's talk about the job.

Some radio stations have news departments equipped with the most sophisticated electronic equipment and the most highly trained personnel in the industry. Others have a microphone that looks like a museum piece, a typewriter that works sometimes, a manager who understands little about journalism, let alone radio journalism, and a disc jockey who thinks news is something to tolerate because it interrupts the record show. If someone were to tell you that you have a better chance making a significant career in radio journalism if you start at the desk with the antique microphone rather than at the modern control center, you would probably say, "Impossible!" You are wrong.

By starting at the antique microphone, you will gain a much broader perspective on radio journalism. You will learn to understand the other programming needs of the station, how the disc jockey thinks, and most important, how management thinks. If you have a positive attitude and learn all you can, you will also play a more important role within the total operation of the station. During the course of a day, you will most likely cover a police beat, a school board meeting, an accident, and you will talk to public officials, write news copy, rewrite news copy, communicate with your wire service bureau, and make decisions about what news will be aired on your radio station. You will experience a microcosm of the total radio world, not just the narrow confines of a small desk in a big newsroom. You will also be a practicing radio journalist and will have the opportunity to meet people, learn your profession, and develop your expertise. If you have energy, ambition, and self-discipline, and if you continually strive for excellence, you will have a good chance of succeeding in the profession.

UNDERSTANDING THE INDUSTRY

Someone once asked, "What ever happened to radio?" When television cameras relayed reports from Far Eastern rice paddies, and when the Watergate scandals elevated two investigative newspaper reporters into prominence, radio seemed to be left out in the cold. Actually, radio journalism was right there all along, reporting what it does best—local news. It's a hometown medium. Although people tune to the national television news each evening and read the paper, they also tune with loyality and interest to the local radio stations. They want to hear how their children were affected by a local school board meeting, how seriously their neighbor was burned in a fire, or how the local judge is holding up under a community political scandal. Radio is a local medium, and it has a loyal local following.

When you mention a job in radio news, some may ask, "What's that?" The reaction is not surprising when you realize that many journalism teachers are products of a newspaper background. Few have had professional experience in broadcast journalism. Because of the excitement of the industry, and because broadcasting is still relatively young, those who have retired from its ranks to teach are few and far between.

All this points to three considerations. First, of all the mass media, the majority of people seeking jobs are not attuned to seeking jobs in radio. Second, much of the preparation for job hunting in radio must be left to the individual. Third, few people are adequately trained for jobs in radio journalism. They may have learned how to write effectively, report effectively, and even take pictures. However, to coordinate the elements of print and sound into a unified communicative entity is a special art and science. By realizing that all of this coordination is necessary, you're one step ahead. What is the next step to your first radio radio news job? We'll start with experience.

GAINING EXPERIENCE

At a recent convention of a state wire service association, students and broadcasters spent two hours together exchanging views on how to land jobs in broadcast journalism. The broadcasters chided students for not obtaining experience before applying for jobs, and the students chided broadcasters for not giving them jobs to gain experience. This stalemate attitude is common among both students and broadcasters, and both are to blame.

The fact remains that when a broadcaster has to decide whether to hire you, working at another radio station will be the most important element on your resume. The call letters of any station will be the most noticed and remembered item. The schools you attended and activities you pursued will take second priority to the listing of your professional experience.

One of the most effective ways to gain experience is through an industry internship program. Some schools have well-developed internship programs and stress them as an important part of training in broadcast journalism. In most cases, media internships are more typical of print rather than broadcast media. If your school does have an internship program, by all means take advantage of it. If you can, participate in more than one internship experience at more than one station.

The advantage of an internship experience is two-fold. First, it permits you to meet people in the broadcasting industry, people who can help you locate a job when you're ready to seek one. You may even be fortunate enough to be hired by your internship station. After all, if you were a manager who needed to hire a radio journalist, you would feel more comfortable hiring someone you knew. Internships can be the big break in landing your first job. Second, even if you don't land a job at your internship station, you still will have gained valuable experience that you can list on your resume.

If your school doesn't have an internship program, take the initiative to gain experience on your own. Contact a radio station in your community and ask if you could spend part of your summer interning there. Don't expect to be paid for the experience, although you might be. The object of an internship is not to earn money but to earn experience, even if you must do it in the evening after a paying summer job.

You can also search out a radio station near your school or home to gain part-time work experience. This can be just as effective as an internship, whether or not you happen to work for the news department of the station. While involved in part-time work, take the time to learn all you can about the operation of the news department. If you can, volunteer your time, work extra hours, and help cover or write news stories. Like the internship, the part-time job will be an impressive item on your resume.

Another way to gain experience is through an educational radio station at your school. Volunteer your time, apply for student positions, and help with the news department's activities. This is legitimate working experience that can be an important plus in your favor.

Few radio station managers have escaped the experience of having a college graduate walk into their office and insinuate that he or she knows it all. Because broadcasting is a relatively new business, most managers worked their way into their positions through hard work and with little more than a high school education. The thought of young college graduates saying they've learned all there is to know about broadcast journalism leaves a sour impression. The lesson of being humble, even if you're a talented genius, is one of the most important lessons you can learn.

PERSONAL CONTACTS

Meeting people in the broadcasting industry is helpful in landing your first job. Although the saying, "It's not what you know but who you know that counts" is not totally accurate, contacts are important. Again, this goes back to the fact that management is more apt to hire people they know.

Where and how do you meet management? One of the best ways is through state press associations. UPI and AP have organizations in every state, and if your college radio station subscribes to one of these wire services, you are entitled to attend state meetings and activities. Also, state broadcast associations usually welcome students at their meetings. Student membership in the various professional organizations mentioned in Chapter 9 entitles you to attend meetings with working professionals on a national level. Don't pass up these opportunities and don't wait until you're ready to seek a job before becoming actively involved.

When you meet these professional broadcasters, it's important to remember their names. During a spare moment, jot down their names, where they work, what their position is, and something unique about them. For instance, during a conversation, you may have learned that a certain station manager likes to fish. If you've jotted this fact down, you can recall it in your introductory letter to him or her; this personal reference may be just the friendly touch needed to open the job door for you.

PREPARING A RESUME

The resume is just a single piece of typed paper, but it communicates *everything* about you. It can mean the difference between never hearing from an employer or being invited to appear for an interview. Every word contributes toward an impression.

There are many different types of resumes. The example in Figure 10A is one which has received positive comments from management. It is concise, direct, and presents the important background information without going into unnecessary detail.

Certain guidelines apply to all resumes. First, make sure your resume is neat and that it's typed *perfectly,* even if this means having it professionally printed. Show your completed rough draft to *at least* three or four other people for their evaluation. Have them check spelling and content. If they feel an item on your resume is confusing, then *change it.* Certain things on your resume may be crystal clear to you but may be unclear to someone else. For example, many colleges and universities have campus organizations with Greek names that mean absolutely nothing to someone who has never belonged to those organizations. The Alpha Alpha Society may be a select group of award-winning broadcast journalists on your campus, but for all a radio station manager knows, it could be a Thursday night poker club. So, be specific. If the type of organization is easily identifiable by the title, such as Society of Professional Journalists, Sigma Delta Chi, then let it stand. If it is something that is not self-explanatory, then label it. You may also want to provide a picture of yourself, although it's certainly not necessary.

Second, be careful to include dates on your resume. Don't simply list the fact that you have received a B.A. degree without listing the date you graduated. Resumes may become part of someone's file for years. People want to know when you completed school. This same advice holds true for your professional experience and other activities.

Third, use a chronological order to your resume, listing the most recent activities first, so that a manager glancing quickly over your resume can pinpoint your progress. However, if you were involved in several activities simultaneously, then it's wise to list the most important activity first, especially those that apply to the job you're seeking. For instance, if you worked at the campus radio station, this information is much more important than your membership in a campus gardening club and should be listed first.

Sometimes the chronological resume may not be the best for your particular needs. If you're a woman, this order accentuates employment gaps you may have had or will have bearing and raising children. The functional resume, on the other hand, enables you to organize your qualifica-

```
                              JANE A. DOE


PRESENT ADDRESS                        PERMANENT ADDRESS

   600 Anderson Avenue                    1 Hilltop Drive
   Laramie, Wyoming  82070                Vernal, Utah  84078
   (307) 766-0000                         (801) 789-0000

PERSONAL DATA

   Born April 7, 1957 in Vernal, Utah.
   Attended the public schools of Vernal, Utah.

EDUCATION

   University of Wyoming, Laramie, Wyoming  82070
      B.A. in Communication, 1977.

PROFESSIONAL EXPERIENCE

   WAZY, Lafayette, Indiana - January, 1977.
      Internship in the news department.  Involved in writing
      and on-air announcing.
   KBOI, Boise, Idaho - January, 1976.
      Internship in the news department.  Assigned as a police
      beat reporter.

ORGANIZATIONAL MEMBERSHIP AND ACTIVITY

   KUWR-FM, University of Wyoming - 1975 to 1977.  Responsible
      for supervising news department personnel and reporting
      local news.
   Society of Professional Journalists, Sigma Delta Chi - 1977-
   Women In Communication, Inc. - 1976-

HONORS AND AWARDS

   Wyoming UPI Broadcasters - Best Radio Documentary - 1976.


   An audition tape is included.  References available upon request.


   5/77
```

Figure 10-A

tions according to skills, rather than to periods of time, and to arrange them in order of importance to your prospective job. With this type of resume, you can eliminate job titles that do not reflect all you did in a particular job and instead write a brief description of the job responsibilities. You should also include a complete list of volunteer and community activities on a functional resume. If you spearheaded your community's

Heart Fund Drive, coordinating the efforts of thousands of people, that shows your prospective employer you have valuable professional skills.

Fourth, be sure to update your resume. If, for example, you prepared a resume and then a month later won a broadcasting award, revise the resume. Don't let it become old.

Fifth, choose your references carefully. People you know well are going to give you a better recommendation than slight acquaintances. Names and titles don't always make the difference. Even though you may be tempted to list the dean of your school as a reference, a professor you've worked closely with will be much more likely to give you an honest, detailed recommendation.

Sixth, include an introductory letter. Keep it neat, like the resume. Take the time to find out the name of the station manager by a quick phone call or a check in *Broadcasting Yearbook,* thus avoiding the impersonal "Dear Sir." Include some personal qualities about yourself and mention why you're interested in a career in radio journalism and why you're applying to that specific station. Form letters abound on any manager's desk, and yours must stand out from the crowd. Show enthusiasm and interest in your letter. Like the resume, the introductory letter is the first impression management will have of you. Whereas the resume is a source of information, the introductory letter *talks* to the manager. It communicates an image of you sitting in the office and carrying on a conversation. Will management enjoy talking to you, or will you just be another person who happens to be taking up time? You're a unique individual; communicate these unique qualities. Without being overbearing, sell yourself!

THE AUDITION TAPE

Just as a radio news story creates an image in the mind of the listener, an audition tape creates an image in the mind of management. That image not only conveys what your voice sounds like, but also how professional your handling of the material is. Your audition tape must stand out from the crowd. It must be a composite of all your radio news abilities; it must show your ability to write, produce, coordinate, and make good news judgments. The audition tape is an individualized work of art to be placed in a specific gallery.

Certain guidelines apply when preparing audition tapes. First, use the very best recording equipment available. Most radio stations are equipped with broadcast-quality equipment. An audition tape spliced and produced on a $100 tape recorder and replayed on professional quality broadcast equipment will sound bad and will reflect negatively on you. It would be much the same as typing your resume with a worn-out typewriter ribbon.

Second, make the audition tape a showcase of your abilities. Don't just sit in front of the microphone and read news copy. Include all of the qualities of a professional newscast—audio actualities, wraparounds, and correspondent reports—*but* don't let these things dominate the newscast. *You* are the one applying for a job, not a series of correspondents.

Third, keep in mind the format and market size of the station to which you're applying and plan your audition tape accordingly. If possible, listen to the station and determine the type of news programming they use; then try to approximate this news format in your audition tape. Don't, for example, cut an audition tape for a contemporary news format and send it to a classical music station.

At the beginning of the tape, record your name, address, and telephone number. This is your insurance policy in case the letter accompanying the tape becomes lost, and the station needs to contact you. In addition, label the outside of the tape with your name, address, and telephone number. Take the time to make more than one audition tape. To lose your master copy after all the work you put into it could be disastrous.

A unique approach one student used to make her audition tape stand out from the rest was to attach a candid snapshot of herself to the front of the tape box. The snapshot showed her at work in a radio news room with radio headphones on, obviously enjoying her work.

After the audition tape is completed, have other people listen to it. The best reviewers are professional broadcasters or your teachers. The main criterion is that someone besides yourself listens to the tape and makes recommendations. Heed those recommendations and don't hesitate to recut the tape if it's not *perfect*. Radio station managers and program directors have an ear for audition tapes, much the same way an artist can visually critique a painting. Your audition tape must be nothing short of superior.

APPEARING FOR AN INTERVIEW

After you have sent your resume and perhaps your audition tape, try to make an appointment for a job interview. A phone call to request an appointment is fine, but appearing in person may be even better. Remember, it's easier to say "no" over the phone than it is face-to-face. Keep in mind that fine line between being persistent and being pushy.

Once you've scheduled an interview at the station's convenience, be prepared to put your best foot forward. This includes being prompt and being prepared. It also includes being well dressed. Management views you not only as the person who can do the job, but also as the person who will represent the station. You will be in public view more than any other member of the staff. As a radio journalist, you will be seen by important public officials as well as business and community leaders. Management is not interested in sending a "soup sandwich" out to meet these people. Therefore, when you're preparing for the interview, pay close attention to those important details of "spit and polish" such as clean hair, shined shoes, clean fingernails, and pressed clothes.

When meeting management people for the first time, greet them by name, if you're sure of the pronunciation. Here again, a quick phone call to the station's receptionist will give you the answer. However, avoid being chummy. Nicknames and first names are out unless you have known that person for a long time. If the manager moves to shake hands, return the action as if you mean it. Shaking hands is appropriate for men as well as women and communicates a positive attitude.

Be prepared for all sorts of questions. Be honest and sincere, but be on your toes. A few favorite openers include, "What can I do for you?" "Tell me about yourself," and "Why are you interested in this station?" Some of the questions may become personal, but for a reason. If you're engaged and a manager asks you how your upcoming marriage will affect your career, you had better be ready with an answer. Equal employment opportunity regulations discourage this type of questions, however. If you are interviewed for a job with a radio station group and reveal that you couldn't stand to live in a certain city, which happens to be the corporate headquarters or the home of one of the other stations in the group, then you may not land the job. If you mention that you hate early mornings or wouldn't accept any job that starts before 7:00 A.M., then you probably won't be working in radio. It's also important to show a willingness to learn. You obviously don't know it all, no matter how much experience you have. People are turned off by inflated egos, so don't display one.

Be prepared to discuss salary. No firm guidelines exist in this area. Federal law prohibits discrimination, and the FCC is very firm in enforcing those regulations. You won't be at a disadvantage because you're a woman or a member of a minority, but you may be at a disadvantage if you insist upon an unreasonably high starting salary. Remember, your first job is your important "foot in the door." You may start with low pay and long hours. The hours come with the job; the pay is most likely based on what you're worth to the station. After all, you have not proven yourself, and management only knows you through a resume and an audition tape. As an unknown, you cannot command either a large salary or the luxury of naming your hiring price. If you are offered the job, you may not be prepared to say "yes" or "no" at that moment. If you're unsure about accepting the job, courteously ask for time to think it over.

Regardless of whether or not you're offered the job, follow up the interview with a prompt, personal thank you letter for the courtesy extended to you. You may also want to express your continued interest. If you don't land that particular job, perhaps another job will open in the future, and your letter of thanks will leave one more positive impression on management.

If you haven't heard anything in a week, follow up with a personal telephone call. The manager may have been called out of town, or something may have developed at the station that postponed a hiring decision. Again, be persistent, but don't be pushy. The difference between the two is an extremely fine line. Basically, use your common sense and judge each situation individually.

YOUR FIRST JOB

Assuming you have landed your first job, your work has just begun. You must now prove yourself through hard work and cooperation. Don't be afraid to volunteer a few overtime hours perfecting your own tasks or learning about other aspects of the station's operation. Take part in station activities, such as special community-sponsored events. By your willingness to work and to cooperate, you will not only gain experience, but you will also gain appreciation and respect.

Above all, take a *positive attitude* toward your work, your station, and your associates. One of the most damaging and immature qualities you can possess is negativism. The label of "pessimist" or "complainer" will follow you throughout your career, assuming you can keep a job long enough to have a career. Negativism can creep into your attitude without your realizing it. You may feel you're working too hard for what you're being paid. Or you may feel the equipment isn't up to par and prevents you from doing your job the way you want to. Keep in mind that these same conditions exist in every job, in every radio station, and in every size market. Say to yourself, "This will really be a challenge," and then put forth the effort to meet that challenge. You will be respected for it and will be able to move to another job with good recommendations.

"MOVIN' ON"

You've learned a great deal from your first job at the small radio station, but now it's time to move on. Although you're fairly professional, your station may not be able to pay you any more money or offer you any advancement. How long you stay at your first job will depend on various factors. Although no hard and fast rule exists, normally three to five years at the same station will insure you a professional foothold in the industry and negate a "job jumping" reputation.

When you do decide to move, make sure the move is not lateral. Your new position should reflect a move upward to more money, a larger market, more responsibilities, new challenges, or an ideal combination of them all. Many small stations are part of a group, and you may have an opportunity to remain with the same company but move to one of the larger stations in the group. Don't be afraid of the unknown. It's easy to grow complacent and secure, but perhaps you want more in life. If you do, reach out for that new horizon, and you're on your way!

Radio journalism has changed enormously since the Harding-Cox election reports first aired on the pioneer voice of KDKA. The medium has matured, and its people have become highly trained and experienced professionals. Radio journalism is an exciting profession and you have an excellent opportunity to become part of it.

SUMMARY

Landing a job in radio news involves foresight and preparation. First, you need to understand the unique nature of the medium and recognize that you'll probably have a better chance of obtaining a job at a small radio station rather than a large one. You'll have a head start by gaining radio news experience through an internship or part-time work. Personal contacts with broadcasting professionals are also valuable.

Important prerequisites in landing a job are a neat, comprehensive resume, an accompanying introductory letter, and a professional-sounding audition tape. Come prepared to put your best foot forward in your job interview. When you land your first job, learn everything you can about the business and perfect your abilities until you reach the point when it's time to move on.

Radio journalism is an exciting profession; welcome to its ranks!

SUGGESTED EXERCISES

1. Consult *Broadcasting Yearbook* for the names of the managers of ten radio stations you might be interested in applying to for a job.

2. Following the example in this chapter, prepare a resume that you would use to apply for a job in radio journalism. Have someone critique your resume. How could it be improved? What opportunities do you have to gain more professional experience to list on your resume?

3. Write a sample introductory letter to a prospective employer. Communicate those qualities of your personality that make you a unique individual.

4. Prepare an audition tape. Include the techniques of radio news production discussed in Chapter 6.

5. With a friend, role-play your first job interview at a radio station. Take the part of both the applicant and the employer.

Appendix

CODE OF BROADCAST NEWS ETHICS
RADIO TELEVISION NEWS DIRECTORS ASSOCIATION

The members of the Radio Television News Directors Association agree that their prime responsibility as newsmen—and that of the broadcasting industry as the collective sponsor of news broadcasting—is to provide to the public they serve a news service as accurate, full and prompt as human integrity and devotion can devise. To that end, they declare their acceptance of the standards of practice here set forth, and their solemn intent to honor them to the limits of their ability.

Article One. The primary purpose of broadcast newsmen—to inform the public of events of importance and appropriate interest in a manner that is accurate and comprehensive—shall override all other purposes.

Article Two. Broadcast news presentations shall be designed not only to offer timely and accurate information, but also to present it in the light of relevant circumstances that give it meaning and perspective. This standard means that news reports, when clarity demands it, will be laid against pertinent factual background; that factors such as race, creed, nationality or prior status will be reported only when they are relevant; that comment or subjective content will be properly identified; and that errors in fact will be promptly acknowledged and corrected.

Article Three. Broadcast newsmen shall seek to select material for newscast solely on their evaluation of its merits as news. This standard means that news will be selected on the criteria of significance, community and regional relevance, appropriate human interest, service to defined audiences. It excludes sensationalism or misleading emphasis in any form; subservience to external or "interested" efforts to influence news selection and presentation, whether from within the broadcasting industry or from without. It requires that such terms as "bulletin" and "flash" be used only when the character of the news justifies them; that bombastic or misleading descriptions of newsroom facilities and personnel be rejected, along with undue use of sound and visual effects; and that promotional or publicity material be sharply scrutinized before use and identified by source or otherwise when broadcast.

Article Four. Broadcast newsmen shall at all times display humane respect for the dignity, privacy and the well-being of persons with whom the news deals.

Article Five. Broadcast newsmen shall govern their personal lives and such nonprofessional associations as may impinge on their professional activities in a manner that will protect them from conflict of interest, real or apparent.

Article Six. Broadcast newsmen shall seek actively to present all news the knowledge of which will serve the public interest, no matter what selfish, uninformed or corrupt efforts attempt to color it, withhold it or prevent its presentation. They shall make constant effort to open doors closed to the reporting of public proceedings with tools appropriate to broadcasting (including cameras and recorders), consistent with the public interest. They acknowledge the newsman's ethic of protection of confidential information and sources, and urge unswerving observation of it except in instances in which it would clearly and unmistakably defy the public interest.

Article Seven. Broadcast newsmen recognize the responsibility borne by broadcasting for informed analysis, comment and editorial opinion on public events and issues. They accept the obligation of broadcasters, for the presentation of such matters by individuals whose competence, experience and judgment qualify them for it.

Article Eight. In court, broadcast newsmen shall conduct themselves with dignity, whether the court is in or out of session. They shall keep broadcast equipment as unobtrusive and silent as possible. Where court facilities are inadequate, pool broadcasts should be arranged.

Article Nine. In reporting matters that are or may be litigated, the newsman shall avoid practices which would tend to interfere with the right of an individual to a fair trial.

Article Ten. Broadcast newsmen shall actively censure and seek to prevent violations of these standards, and shall actively encourage their observance by all newsmen, whether of the Radio Television News Directors Association or not.

NATIONAL ASSOCIATION OF BROADCASTERS RADIO CODE

Program Standards: News

Radio is unique in its capacity to reach the largest number of people first with reports on current events. This competitive advantage bespeaks caution—being first is not as important as being accurate. The Radio Code standards relating to the treatment of news and public events are, because of constitutional considerations, intended to be exhortatory. The standards set forth hereunder encourage high standards of professionalism in broadcast journalism. They are not to be interpreted as turning over to others the broadcaster's responsibility as to judgments necessary in news and public events programming.

1. News Sources. Those responsible for news on radio should exercise constant professional care in the selection of sources—on the premise that the integrity of the news and the consequent good reputation of radio as a dominant well-balanced news medium depend largely upon the reliability of such sources.

2. News Reporting. News reporting should be factual, fair and without bias. Good taste should prevail in the selection and handling of news. Morbid, sensational, or alarming details not essential to factual reporting should be avoided. News should be broadcast in such a manner as to avoid creation of panic and unnecessary alarm. Broadcasters should be diligent in their supervision of content, format, and presentation of news broadcasts. Equal diligence should be exercised in selection of editors and reporters who direct news gathering and dissemination, since the station's performance in this vital informational field depends largely upon them.

3. Commentaries and Analyses. Special obligations devolve upon those who analyze and/or comment upon news developments, and management should be satisfied completely that the task is to be performed in the best interest of the listening public. Programs of news analysis and commentary should be clearly identified as such, distinguishing them from straight news reporting.

4. Editorializing. Broadcasts in which stations express their own opinions about issues of general public interest should be clearly identified as editorials.

5. Coverage of News and Public Events. In the coverage of news and public events broadcasters should exercise their judgments consonant with the accepted standards of ethical journalism and should provide accurate, informed and adequate coverage.

6. Placement of Advertising. Broadcasters should exercise particular discrimination in the acceptance, placement and presentation of advertising in news programs so that such advertising is clearly distinguishable from the news content.

THE SOCIETY OF PROFESSIONAL JOURNALISTS,
SIGMA DELTA CHI
CODE OF ETHICS

The Society of Professional Journalists, Sigma Delta Chi, believes the duty of journalists is to serve the truth.

We believe the agencies of mass communication are carriers of public discussion and information, acting on their Constitutional mandate and freedom to learn and report the facts.

We believe in public enlightenment as the forerunner of justice, and in our Constitutional role to seek the truth as part of the public's right to know the truth.

We believe those responsibilities carry obligations that require journalists to perform with intelligence, objectivity, accuracy, and fairness.

To these ends, we declare acceptance of the standards of practice here set forth:

Responsibility. The public's right to know of events of public importance and interest is the overriding mission of the mass media. The purpose of distributing news and enlightened opinion is to serve the general welfare. Journalists who use their professional status as representatives of the public for selfish or other unworthy motives violate a high trust.

Freedom of the Press. Freedom of the press is to be guarded as an inalienable right of people in a free society. It carries with it the freedom and the responsibility to discuss, question, and challenge actions and utterances of our government and of our public and private institutions. Journalists uphold the right to speak unpopular opinions and the privilege to agree with the majority.

Ethics. Journalists must be free of obligation to any interest other than the public's right to know the truth.

1. Gifts, favors, free travel, special treatment or privileges can compromise the integrity of journalists and their employers. Nothing of value should be accepted.

2. Secondary employment, political involvement, holding public office, and service in community organizations should be avoided if it compromises the integrity of journalists and their employers. Journalists and their employers should conduct their personal lives in a manner which protects them from conflict of interest, real or apparent. Their responsibilities to the public are paramount. That is the nature of their profession.

3. So-called news communications from private sources should not be published or broadcast without substantiation of their claims to news value.

4. Journalists will seek news that serves the public interest, despite the obstacles. They will make constant efforts to assure that the public's business is conducted in public and that public records are open to public inspection.

5. Journalists acknowledge the newsman's ethic of protecting confidential sources of information.

Accuracy and Objectivity. Good faith with the public is the foundation of all worthy journalism.

1. Truth is our ultimate goal.

2. Objectivity in reporting the news is another goal, which serves as the mark of an experienced professional. It is a standard of performance toward which we strive. We honor those who achieve it.

3. There is no excuse for inaccuracies or lack of thoroughness.

4. Newspaper headlines should be fully warranted by the contents of the articles they accompany. Photographs and telecasts should give an accurate picture of an event and not highlight a minor incident out of context.

5. Sound practice makes clear distinction between news reports and expressions of opinion. News reports should be free of opinion or bias and represent all sides of an issue.

6. Partisanship in editorial comment which knowingly departs from the truth violates the spirit of American journalism.

7. Journalists recognize their responsibility for offering informed analysis, comment, and editorial opinion on public events and issues. They accept the obligation to present such material by individuals whose competence, experience, and judgment qualify them for it.

8. Special articles or presentations devoted to advocacy or the writer's own conclusions and interpretations should be labeled as such.

Fair Play. Journalists at all times will show respect for the dignity, privacy, rights, and well-being of people encountered in the course of gathering and presenting the news.

1. The news media should not communicate unofficial charges affecting reputation or moral character without giving the accused a chance to reply.

2. The news media must guard against invading a person's right to privacy.

3. The media should not pander to morbid curiosity about details of vice and crime.

4. It is the duty of news media to make prompt and complete correction of their errors.

5. Journalists should be accountable to the public for their reports and the public should be encouraged to voice its grievances against the media. Open dialogue with our readers, viewers, and listeners should be fostered.

Pledge. Journalists should actively censure and try to prevent violations of these standards, and they should encourage their observance by all newspeople. Adherence to this code of ethics is intended to preserve the bond of mutual trust and respect between American journalists and the American people.

NATIONAL ASSOCIATION OF BROADCASTERS
STANDARDS OF CONDUCT FOR BROADCASTING
PUBLIC PROCEEDINGS *

Broadcast newsmen are devoted guardians of our priceless heritage of freedom. They are particularly concerned with safeguarding freedom of speech and freedom of communications. They believe that the surest way to preserve these freedoms is to exercise them with vigor. They recognize that the vigorous exercise of freedom must be carried forward with a decent respect for the rights and opinions of others and for the established procedures of public agencies, judicial, legislative, and executive.

Public Hearings and Meetings

In keeping with these principles, broadcast newsmen, special events broadcasters, film cameramen and technical personnel who work with them will conduct themselves at public hearings in accordance with the following standards:

They will conform to the established procedures, customs, and decorum of the legislative halls, hearing rooms, and other public places where they provide broadcast coverage of public business.

At all public hearings they will respect the authority of the presiding officer to make appropriate rules of order and conduct.

Coverage arrangements will make maximum use of modern techniques for unobtrusive installation and operation of broadcasting equipment. Coverage will be pooled where necessary. Call letters should not be displayed in case of multiple coverage.

In those many instances where commercial sponsorship of news coverage of public proceedings is desirable on economic grounds, commercials will be in good taste and will be clearly separated from the news content of the program. Broadcasters, of course, will honor to the letter any agreements with the presiding official regarding sponsorship.

Newsmen will present summaries of the proceedings, and will conduct interviews, or broadcast commentaries only during recesses, or outside the hearing room, or during appropriate portions of other proceedings in a manner that will assure that the broadcast does not distract from the public business.

---

* Adopted by Freedom of Information Committee and Board of Directors, National Association of Broadcasters.

In the Courtroom

The sanctity of public trial and the rights of the defendant and all parties require that special care be exercised to assure that broadcast coverage will in no way interfere with the dignity and decorum and the proper and fair conduct of such proceedings. In recognition of the paramount objective of justice inherent in all trials, broadcast newsmen will observe the following standards:

They will abide by all rules of the court.

The presiding judge is, of course, recognized as the appropriate authority, and broadcast newsmen will address their applications for admission to him and will conform to his rulings. The right to appeal to higher jurisdiction is reserved.

Broadcast equipment will be installed in a manner acceptable to the court and will be unobtrusively located and operated so as not to be disturbing or distracting to the court or participants.

Broadcast newsmen will not move about while court is in session in such a way as to interfere with the orderly proceedings. Their equipment will remain stationary.

Commentaries on the trial will not be broadcast from the courtroom while the trial is in session.

Broadcasting of trials will be presented to the community as a public service, and there will be no commercial sponsorship of such trials.

Broadcast personnel will dress in accordance with courtroom custom.

Index